THE INVESTITURE CONTROVERSY

Ruins of the castle of Canossa in the Emilian Apennines. (*Tourist office, province of Reggio Emilia*)

THE INVESTITURE CONTROVERSY

Issues, Ideals, and Results

Edited by **KARL F. MORRISON**
The University of Chicago

HOLT, RINEHART AND WINSTON
New York • Chicago • San Francisco • Atlanta
Dallas • Montreal • Toronto • London • Sydney

Cover illustration: *(Above)* Gregory VII is expelled
from Rome by Henry IV, who is seated with antipope
Guibert. *(Below)* Gregory excommunicates Henry's
clergy and dies in exile. From the *Chronicle* of Otto
of Freising, twelfth century. *(The Granger Collection)*

CONTENTS

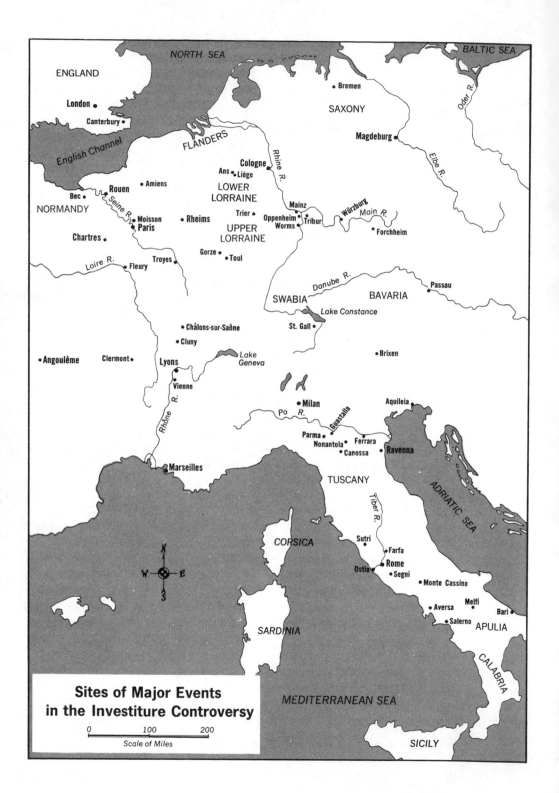

**Sites of Major Events
in the Investiture Controversy**

0   100   200
Scale of Miles

CHRONOLOGY

1049–54 POPE LEO IX. The reform began. The most influential figures at the papal court were Peter Damiani, Cardinal Humbert of Silva Candida, and Hildebrand (later Pope Gregory VII).

1049 Synods of Rheims and Mainz, under Leo IX's presidency. Decrees against simony and Nicolaitism.

1054–57 POPE VICTOR II. Hildebrand became dominant in the fiscal and legal activities of the papacy.

1056 Henry IV acceded as German king. When he came to the throne, Henry was five years old, and neither he nor the regencies set up to rule until he came of age could prevent the decay of royal power in Germany.

1057–58 POPE STEPHEN IX

1057–59 Dispute in Milan over simony and Nicolaitism.

1058–61 POPE NICHOLAS II

1059 A Lateran synod prohibited lay investiture and ordered stringent moral reform of the clergy in Rome. Nicholas II promulgated his Papal Election Decree, which gave the new College of Cardinals the dominant role in electing popes. Its ambiguous provisions concerning the traditional role of the German king in papal accessions paved the way to dispute.

1059 A synod of Melfi prohibited clerical marriage or concubinage and led to the alliance of the papacy with the Normans of southern Italy.

1061–73 POPE ALEXANDER II

1061 The German court contested Alexander's election, arguing that he had been consecrated as bishop of Rome before his election had been approved by Henry IV or his agents, as required by the Papal Election Decree (1059). It set up the Antipope Honorius II (Bishop Cadalous of Parma). The court soon accepted Alexander as true pope for diplomatic reasons, though Cadalous continued to press his claims until his death.

1065–76 Renewed dispute in Milan over simony and Nicolaitism. This was sharpened in 1071–1075 by a contested election to the archbishopric in which Henry IV supported one candidate and the popes, the other.

1066 Henry IV began his personal rule. His main object was to restore royal power over lay vassals and church property.

1070   Odo of Châtillon (future Pope Urban II) was monk, later prior, at
            Cluny.
1073–85   POPE GREGORY VII
1073   Henry IV began to put down an insurrection in Saxony.
1074   Gregory VII's first Lenten synod, in Rome, declared sacraments
            performed by simoniacs or Nicolaites invalid.
1075   Gregory VII's second Lenten synod, in Rome, forbade lay investiture.
1076   The Synod of Worms, on Henry IV's complaint, declared Gregory
            VII deposed.
            In retaliation, Gregory VII's third Lenten synod, in Rome, declared
            Henry IV excommunicated and deposed. Saxon rebels and their
            supporters threatened, at the Diet of Tribur, to elect another king
            unless Henry secured absolution from the Pope before February
            22, 1077.
1077   January 18—After a display of penitence, Henry received absolution
            and communion from Gregory at Canossa. The Pope argued that
            Henry's full restoration to kingly powers had to wait for further
            judgment by Gregory and the Germans. Henry, however, ignored
            this provision and acted as king; and the rebels elected Rudolf of
            Swabia to succeed him (Diet of Forcheim). Gregory remained offi-
            cially neutral toward the civil war in Germany.
1078   Odo of Châtillon (future Pope Urban II) was called to Rome, raised to
            cardinalate, and employed as papal legate.
1080   Henry gained in Saxony and again menaced Gregory VII. At his
            Lenten synod, the Pope excommunicated and deposed Henry for
            the second time, and accepted Rudolf conditionally as king.
            The Synod of Brixen, under Henry's influence, declared Gregory
            deposed and elected Archbishop Guibert of Ravenna as the Anti-
            pope Clement III.
            Rudolf was killed in the battle of the Elster.
1081–84   Henry IV invaded Italy and intermittently besieged Rome.
1083–84   Henry IV took Rome. Guibert was formally installed as pope and
            crowned Henry as emperor. Papal allies, the Normans of southern
            Italy, invaded Rome and sacked the city, rescuing Gregory VII from
            the Castel' Sant' Angelo and taking him to Salerno. A large part of the
            College of Cardinals rejected and abandoned Gregory.
1085   Gregory VII died in Salerno.
1086–87   POPE VICTOR III
1086   Countess Mathilda of Tuscany's first donation of lands to the papacy.
1088–99   POPE URBAN II. The Pope allied with Welf of Bavaria and arranged
            Welf's marriage with Mathilda of Tuscany in an effort to block Henry
            IV from Italy.
            Henry reinvaded Italy and established Clement III in Rome.
1089   Lanfranc of Canterbury died.
1093   William II, of England, forced Abbot Anselm of Bec to accept investi-
            ture and consecration as Archbishop of Canterbury.

1093–1101   Under Urban's encouragement, Henry IV's son and heir-designate Conrad rebelled and gained support in much of Lombardy.

1094   Distracted by Conrad's revolt, Henry could no longer keep Clement III in Rome. The Antipope fled. Urban took the Lateran Palace, the first Gregorian to hold it since 1084.

After largely ending the schism among the cardinals that began under Gregory VII, Urban set out on a two-year journey to gain support in northern Italy and in France.

Urban renewed the excommunication of Henry IV.

1094   The dispute between Anselm of Canterbury and William Rufus began.

1095   Council of Clermont. Urban II proclaimed the First Crusade, thus reasserting the pope's role as general head of Christendom.

Welf of Bavaria repudiated his marriage with Mathilda of Tuscany on grounds of nonconsummation. This weakened the papal position in Germany.

1097   Anselm of Canterbury took refuge at the court of Urban II, and William Rufus seized the revenues of Canterbury.

1099–1118   POPE PASCHAL II

1100   On William Rufus' death, Henry I recalled Anselm. When Henry insisted on the right to reinvest Anselm with the temporalities of Canterbury, Anselm declined, and furthermore, he refused to consecrate bishops-elect who had received lay investiture. The dispute festered.

1102   Paschal II renewed the excommunication of Henry IV. For the second time, Countess Mathilda of Tuscany made a large cession of land to the papacy.

1103–06   Exile of Anselm of Canterbury.

1104–06   Revolt of Henry V, with papal support, against his father, Henry IV.

1106   Henry IV died, still unreconciled with the papacy. At the Synod of Guastalla, Paschal II set forth a tentative compromise: he accepted as legitimate prelates all those whom Henry IV and Henry V had installed by lay investiture, and at the same time he renewed the decrees against simony and lay investiture. This marked a great departure from the rigid policies of Gregory VII and Urban II, and forecast the concessions of 1111. The imperial ambassadors asserted ambiguously "all the rights of the Empire."

Reconciliation of Anselm of Canterbury with Henry I of England.

1107   Paschal II presided at the Synod of Troyes. Henry V's ambassadors asserted that the king had the right to elect and invest bishops on the spurious ground that popes had granted it to Charlemagne. A year's truce was agreed upon at the end of which, it was understood, Henry had to defend his case in Rome.

Agreement of London (Settlement of Bec). The English dispute ended with agreement on three points: (1) that elections of bishops and abbots would not be free and canonical choices by clergy and people but nominations by the king with the advice of "religious persons";

(2) that the persons nominated would, before consecration, do homage to the king for temporalities; and (3) that consecration, with the bestowal of ring and crozier by bishops, would follow homage.

1110	Henry V at last entered Italy.
1111	Under duress, Paschal II issued two decrees, called *privilegia,* in order to reach a settlement with Henry V. In the first, on the understanding that Henry gave up the empty form of lay investiture, he renounced those lands, offices, and rights that the Church held in tenure from the Empire. When this agreement was read in public, it was immediately denounced and Henry took Paschal into protective custody. In the second decree, issued when Paschal was captive in Henry's camp, the Pope accepted the principle of lay investiture. Paschal crowned Henry as emperor.
1112	Lateran Synod. The strong rejection of both *privilegia,* and particularly of the second, led to their nullification. The Synod of Vienne, under Guy of Vienne (future Pope Calixtus II), excommunicated Henry V, declared lay investiture a heresy, and threatened to repudiate obedience to Paschal II if he failed to ratify its decrees.
1115	Despite her cessions to the papacy (1086, 1102) Countess Mathilda of Tuscany on dying left her affairs in such a state that Henry V was able to claim to be lawful heir to her vast lands.
1116	Lateran Synod. Paschal II was forced to repudiate the second *privilegium* again and to confirm the excommunication of Henry V.
1116–17	Henry V invaded Italy to take possession of the Mathildine lands and demanded revocation of papal decrees against him.
1117	When Henry advanced on Rome, Paschal withdrew to Benevento. Henry took Rome, celebrated a triumphant entry, and withdrew.
1118	Paschal II died.
1118–19	POPE GELASIUS II. At Gelasius's surreptitious election by the Gregorians, Henry V invaded Rome, put Gelasius to flight, and installed Archbishop Maurice of Braga as the Antipope Gregory VIII.
1119	Gelasius II died at Cluny.
1119–24	POPE CALIXTUS II
1119	Calixtus held a synod in Rheims which prohibited simony and lay investiture and excommunicated Henry V and Gregory VIII, absolving Henry's subjects of their obedience to him. An interview between Calixtus's representatives and Henry, near Moisson, while the synod was in progress failed to produce a settlement.
1120	Calixtus captured Gregory VIII, whose cruel humiliation was part of Calixtus's triumphant reentry into Rome.
1121	Diet of Würzburg. Henry and his princes concluded a settlement which laid the basis for the Concordat of Worms.
1122	Concordat of Worms. Henry V surrendered to God, St. Peter, and the Church the right to invest prelates with ring and crozier; he conceded to all churches in the Empire the right to free and canonical

elections; he restored to the Church of Rome and all other churches and nobles whatever lands and rights had been lost because of the Investiture Controversy and promised to aid in gaining restitutions; and finally, he granted to the Pope and his supporters peace and . aid to the Church of Rome in all things.

Calixtus II granted to Henry that all elections of bishops and abbots in the Empire should take place in the presence of Henry or his representatives, without simony or violence. (Disputed elections were to be tried by the competent metropolitan and comprovincial bishops.) In Germany, Henry or his agents were to invest bishops-elect with the temporalities (except those held from Rome) by a touch of the scepter, and the prelates were to render all licit services for the rights in question. In other parts of the Empire, temporalities were to be granted within six months after consecration. Finally, the Pope granted Henry and his followers peace and all licit aid.

The papal legate gave Henry communion, declared him reconciled with Rome, and received him and his adherents back into the ortho-dox church.

1123   The First Lateran Council ratified the Concordat of Worms and issued new reform legislation.

INTRODUCTION

Historians interpret differently many fundamental aspects of medieval civilization, but by all odds the Investiture Controversy is the hardiest perennial in the medievalists' garden of debate. The broad course of the dispute is not contested. During the tenth and early eleventh centuries monastic reform movements in France and Germany revived the study of Church law. From 1049 on, a series of German popes began to apply the moral and legal principles of these movements to the clergy at large. They insisted that two canonical abuses especially had led to the moral debasement of the clergy and the resulting withdrawal of laymen from the organized Church: Nicolaitism (the marriage or concubinage of clergy) and simony (purchase of Church offices or sacraments, whether by money or by illicit obligations).

In striving to uproot these practices and restore what they considered canonical order, the reformer-popes forbade lay investiture. It had long been normal and approved by ecclesiastical authority for lay magnates to install newly elected prelates in the secular rights and possessions of their churches. The magnates did this in their role as protectors of the churches, but in practice they turned the right to invest into the power to appoint, subverted the process of canonical election, and either sold the offices to the highest bidder or selected men on whom they could count for political or fiscal support in the future. The reformer-popes considered this abuse a form of simony. They objected most vigorously to the fact that in investing bishops lay magnates bestowed the symbols of the episcopal office, the ring and the crozier, sometimes with the words, "Receive thy church." The impression could hardly be avoided that laymen were conferring not merely worldly rights and possessions but even the spiritual powers of the episcopacy, and that the ritual of consecration, which purported to confer the gifts of the Holy Ghost on prelates-elect, was a mere formality. The reformer-popes solemnly prohibited lay investiture a number of times before the accession of Pope Gregory VII (1073).

Gregory's attack on it produced unprecedented consequences. All the broad purposes of the reform now crystallized around this one issue. Henry IV, the German king, considered Gregory's decree against lay investiture (1075) an attempt to subvert his authority over the episcopacy, one of the mainstays of royal

1

power. He convened a synod which declared Gregory deposed; the Pope retal-
iated with a decree of excommunication and deposition against Henry. Thus began the great controversy.

It lasted for nearly fifty years, until the Concordat of Worms (1122); but, except for one brief though intense conflict in England, the principal actors remained the popes and the German kings; the major issue, the ambiguous duties
of the clergy, as members of the Church, to the papacy and, as subjects, to their
kings; the chief instruments, the law of the canons and zeal for moral regeneration. The main events throughout the dispute are well known and incontestable;
the reader may find them inventoried in the chronology.

It may therefore seem paradoxical that modern historians have failed to
agree as to the origins, issues, and results of the struggle. Were the reformers
revolutionaries—as Henry IV and his partisans thought, though they did not
know the word revolution—in overturning a licit, conventional, and beneficent
order? Were they conservatives—as they themselves held—in brushing aside the
perversions of recent times and restoring the ancient law of the Church? The final
verdict has still to come in. This is the crux of modern scholarly debate. The reason for disagreement lies chiefly in the sources.

The Investiture Controversy gave birth to propaganda. Appeals went not to
society at large but to princes and to clergy, especially those in high offices. The
public addressed was thus narrow and elite, but the critical facts are that for the
first time in postclassical Europe two warring factions enlisted support from beyond the walls of their own strongholds; that this effort took the form of documen-
tary warfare; and that our knowledge of the Controversy rests largely on this
biased and polemical literature. Official letters of kings and popes shook off
stately detachment and took on the distorting color of recrimination. Serious and
well-informed chroniclers deliberately misled by invective. Not only the "lunatic
fringe" on each side but even synods of bishops hatched squalid, untruthful di-
atribes.

The effects of this are clear in assessments of the major figure in the dispute.
Gregory VII dominated the conflict. It was in a sense his controversy, for his
deposition of Henry IV generated the whole series of events that drove Gregory
himself to death in exile, permanently weakened the German monarchy, and
split the English church. What considerations brought Gregory to issue his unprecedented, fateful decree?

Historians differ in their specific explanations. Some detect naked lust for
power; others, zeal for moral reform; still others, outrage at Henry's deliberate
affronts to the dignity of the papal office. But all deductions such as these fall into
two general classes. One view holds that Gregory was a fanatic, a man of demonic
force who consciously sought revolution. In the words of H. H. Milman, "Gregory is the Caesar of spiritual conquest."[1] The other maintains that the Pope's
whole purpose was conservative: His profound, mystical piety led him to insist

---

[1] *History of Latin Christianity* (New York, 1860), vol. 3, p. 497.

that the spiritual regeneration of the Church depended on enforcing the ancient rules of the Fathers. Only in this way could Christians regain the means of salvation which Christ had established and onto which evil practices had impinged. In an exceptional crisis his reverence for ancient authorities led him to carry the letter of the law beyond all precedent by deposing Henry.

Opposition between these two broad attitudes has raised fundamental questions. Did Gregory frame the ideas expressed in deposing Henry and elaborated during the long course of the dispute, or did he merely enact earlier principles of Church reform, especially those espoused by one monastic order, the Cluniac? Was his goal moral regeneration or political power, power for the papacy to judge kings and depose the unworthy? Did the course of events he set in motion end in triumph or defeat for the papacy? The sources yield clear but mutually exclusive answers.

These are the issues to which scholars turned, particularly in the nineteenth and early twentieth century. The best historical standards of that day set a high value on the power of great men to shape civilization. As Thomas Carlyle put it, "Universal history, the history of what man has accomplished in this world, is at bottom the history of the great men who have worked here. . . . All things that we see standing accomplished in the world are properly the outer material result, the practical realization and embodiment of thoughts that dwelt in the great men sent into the world."[2] The emphasis on Gregory's personality—his sources of inspiration, his intent and motives, and his original contribution to the dispute— reflects this attitude.

Discussing the Controversy in terms of personality, however, led historians to look tentatively beyond the great figures to their social and intellectual environments. In evaluating Gregory's originality, or lack of it, monastic reform movements and the revival of legal studies had to be investigated. To understand what drove Henry IV to irremediable obstinacy, one had to grasp the political structure of the German kingdom and the ties between each element in it and the papacy.

By the time of World War I, emphasis lay less on personalities than on the social and intellectual matrix of the dispute. Publications by two authors after World War I gave impetus to this shift. One of these was Erich Caspar, who edited the register of Gregory VII's official letters.[3] The other was Augustin Fliche, who attracted Caspar's disapproval by some essays published as preliminaries to his magisterial study, *La Réforme grégorienne*.[4] The old questions recurred. Caspar argued that Gregory was a highly original thinker, and he took issue with Fliche's shorter essays, which maintained that Gregory had derived his guiding views from other reformers. Still, the general effect of Caspar's edition and Fliche's analysis was to turn studies toward historical context and away from personality.

---

[2] *Heroes, Hero Worship and the Heroic in History* (New York, n.d.), pp. 1 f.
[3] *Das Register Gregors VII.* Berlin, 1920–1923.
[4] Three volumes, Louvain-Paris, 1924–1927.

What did the Controversy reveal about the general character of medieval civilization? What did it contribute to the evolution of Europe? Was it fraught with importance for church-state relations and for the growth of the papal monarchy? Or, in view of the surrender to royal interests in the Agreement of London and of an anticlimactic and virtually inconsequential Concordat of Worms, was it in the long run a protracted error, a trivial episode? These are questions on which scholarly attention now focuses.

Without denying Gregory VII's pivotal role, the tendency of recent studies has been to draw attention to the later stages of the Controversy, after Gregory's death, and to examine the conflict as expressing in a special way both practical difficulties of administrative jurisdiction and a broad development of thought about relations between the Church hierarchy and temporal government, about the social and moral functions of the Church, and about Church order. Looking backward from the dispute, some scholars have seen that the parties to the Controversy were locked into social and political systems as old as the Germanic invasions and that they invoked legal sanctions that the Church Fathers had framed in the last years of the Roman Empire. Looking forward, other scholars have shown that the moral and political crises of the Controversy inspired, on the one hand, diplomatic realignments that led to the Babylonian Captivity of the popes in Avignon in the fourteenth century and, on the other, intellectual positions that prepared the way for the fully developed theories of the late Middle Ages, among them the contrary doctrines of representative government and absolutism.

And yet, through these recent studies runs, unresolved, the persistent question: Was the Investiture Controversy—that is, were the Gregorian doctrines and acts that impelled the dispute—revolutionary or conservative? The familiar riddle of Gregory VII's personality goes unresolved. Applied to the entire circle of Gregorian reformers and their work through fifty years of conflict, the question evokes similar diversity of opinion. One can find tidily polarized positive and negative positions. Norman F. Cantor has concluded that the Gregorians precipitated the first "world-revolution" and that their aim was "not the reform of the prevailing system, but rather its abolition and replacement by a new order."[5] On the same evidence, Walter Ullmann assures us that the Gregorians merely enacted doctrines of Church order, a "hierocratic theme" or system of thought, that had been commonly and steadily acknowledged for centuries before the eleventh century.[6]

There is an astonishing continuity between these recent, hotly contested positions and nineteenth-century judgments. As Caspar wrote in 1924, "At first glance it could seem a rash undertaking to say something new today about Gregory VII."[7] Compare Cantor's words with those of Ferdinand Gregorovius, the great historian of medieval Rome: "[Gregory VII's] importance consisted in the

---

[5] *Church, Kingship and Lay Investiture in England: 1089–1135* (Princeton, N.J., 1958), p. 7.

[6] *The Growth of Papal Government in the Middle Ages,* 2d ed. London, 1962.

[7] "Gregor VII. in seinen Briefen." *Historische Zeitschrift,* 130 (1924), p. 1.

fact that he remodelled the hitherto existing relations of the Church to the world and the temporal power by one of the most violent revolutions known to history. He was the Caesar of papal Rome."[8] Likewise, compare Ullmann's view with that of Abel François Villemain, a distinguished historian and man of letters: "In the earliest advances of pontifical power, we shall find the principle of all that Gregory VII afterwards attempted; and, after the lapse of ages, we shall see that extraordinary man appear, at the head of that sacerdotal empire, which, having been begun before him by the enthusiasm, the fraud, the daring, or the ignorance, or the wants of peoples, maintained itself after him, by the same causes, strengthened by the example his genius had left."[9]

The selections in the following pages reflect the unresolved, perhaps irresoluble, tension between the positions. In all aspects of the Controversy, we shall find them at odds, as they have been since the day the tumultuous Romans acclaimed a grieving Hildebrand as pope.

In the present work the chronology and the essays in the section on the contours of the dispute have been included to guide the student through the historical labyrinth of the conflict. Z. N. Brooke describes with beautiful lucidity the legal issues; Paul Joachimsen, the political state of Germany which gave the conflict special ferocity there; and Demetrius B. Zema, the material vulnerability of the papacy.

The remaining sections are designed to reveal the central ambiguities of the conflict. On Gregory VII as traditionalist or innovator, the texts and the essays by Gerhart B. Ladner and Karl F. Morrison show that the strands of revolution and conservatism are tightly woven together and almost inseparable, even to the eye of the specialist.

Did Paschal II's breathtaking abandonment of all that the reformers had fought for represent a recovery of moral strength or a confession of political impotence? Ferdinand Gregorovius and Peter R. McKeon stand on different sides.

Finally, who won? Polarization of opinion could hardly be clearer than in the statement by James Bryce that the papacy won unconditionally, and that by Arnold J. Toynbee that it lost absolutely. With regard to the related dispute in England, John Tracy Ellis stands at the third point of a triangle, saying that the king won. In the balanced spirit of compromise, Robert L. Benson takes the middle position, asserting that each party gained something.

It is hoped that students may be able to draw conclusions of their own from the translations of some essential texts.

---

[8] *History of the City of Rome in the Middle Ages,* translated by Annie Hamilton (London, 1896), vol. 4, pt. 1, p. 167.
[9] *Life of Gregory VII,* translated by J. B. Brockley, (London, 1874) vol. 1, p. 2.

In the reprinted selections footnotes appearing in the original sources have in general been omitted unless they contribute to the argument or better understanding of the selection.

Apart from four years as an artilleryman and two further years in the military intelligence corps (1914–1919), Z. N. BROOKE (1883–1946) lived in the peaceful confines of Cambridge University. His wide learning and clarity of thought earned great respect among scholars and brought him to the joint-editorship of the *Cambridge Medieval History*. Ill health in later life prevented him from completing his ambitious project for a comprehensive history of the Gregorian reform movement. *The English Church and the Papacy* (1931) shows the intellectual power that might have been brought to the larger work; it was also remarkable as the earliest attempt to examine, on manuscript evidence, the impact of canon law studies on the English church in the eleventh and twelfth centuries.*

Z. N. Brooke

The Issue of Law:
Conflict of Churches

I have made it sufficiently evident that, when I speak of the English Church, I understand the phrase to connote nothing more than that part of the Church which was constituted in England. I do not deny that it had a certain definite unity of its own, since the Papacy, by adopting this territorial nomenclature, recognised it as a constituent part of the whole Church. But we must be careful to appreciate the character of this unity, and not to attribute to it something that it only acquired at a much later date. The unity was of a secular and not of an ecclesiastical character, and was only an expression of the fact that all its members were the subjects of one king. So, too, the Norman Church had a distinct unity, in that all its members were the subjects of one duke. The fact that king and duke were the same man did not unite the two Churches. Secular conditions, which gave each Church its unity, kept the two Churches separate, even though the Norman Church supplied the English with most of its bishops and abbots; they ceased to be members of the Norman and became members of the English Church. Elsewhere this is equally true. We can speak of the German Church or the French Church (of which the Norman was in a sense a part) to imply that part of the Church situated in the territories ruled by the king of Germany or the king of France. And, as I have said, the control of the lay rulers over the Church in their dominions was such that the Popes could not ignore it; accordingly, when they sent out legates, espe-

*From Z. N. Brooke, *The English Church and the Papacy from the Conquest to the Reign of John* (Cambridge, Eng.: Cambridge University Press, 1931), pp. 22–31, 41–43. Footnotes omitted.

cially standing legates, they commonly allocated as their sphere a whole kingdom; they sent them to Germany, to France, or to England.

However, these divisions, though used for ecclesiastical purposes, were really only secular. Ecclesiastically, the Church was a unity, "the undivided garment of Christ," divided for purposes of administration into provinces and sees; and its provinces did not always coincide with the secular divisions. In the eleventh century there was nobody in England, or elsewhere, who questioned the essential unity of the Church, or denied that it was under papal headship. This is certainly true of England after the Conquest, when William I brought the English Church back again into line with the Church as a whole, and it is for this reason that I have chosen the Conquest as the point from which to commence this enquiry. The Conquest does mark, in essentials, such a clean sweep with the past. Not only the new secular ruler, but also the new ecclesiastical officials, came from the Continent. During Edward the Confessor's reign, foreigners had been introduced, but there was great hostility to them. Now they are imposed without effective resistance everywhere, and it is some time before an Englishman has a chance of promotion in the English Church. It is particularly the Church that is affected by one of the principal results of the Conquest—the renewed connection with the Continent. The Church is reorganised and governed by foreigners, in accordance with the ideas that they brought with them from the Continent.

On the other hand, William acted as the master of the Church in England, and took careful measures to interpose a barrier in order to prevent the intrusion of papal authority. To say that he brought it into line with the Church, and then that

he kept it as a Church apart, seems at first sight a manifest contradiction in terms. Yet when we regard the general history of the Church, we can see that there is no contradiction or even inconsistency in his attitude. It is only, as I insisted at the beginning, by commencing with the history of the Church as a whole, that we can view in its true perspective the history of that part of the Church which was in England.

The eleventh century is, in Church history, the great century of reform, and it divides into two quite distinct halves. Before 1046, when the Papacy was still unreformed, the Church as a whole had no leader, and only a nominal head. The papal primacy was, indeed, generally acknowledged, though the scandals of the papal court had ruined its prestige and discredited its authority. The Roman Church was still the one from which authority was derived, and it had long been customary for archbishops to apply to the Pope for their pallia, and many monasteries based their privileges on papal charters; it had long been looked to as an authority to give a ruling on difficult questions of law, or as an arbitrator in important disputes. But when it departed from this passive rôle to take the initiative, when it tried to exert its authority over an archbishop or a bishop, it was strongly and successfully resisted, and it had no means of enforcing its orders. Its position was not unlike that of the king of France, whose overlordship was recognised, though the great vassals usually disregarded his authority and only recognised it when it was of advantage to themselves, as for instance when they wished for the settlement of a legal dispute with one of their peers. The analogy is useful, because William I was one of these vassals of the king of France.

The Reform Movement, then, in the

first half of the century was quite independent of the Pope and was under no
single direction. It therefore took many
forms. Cluny had concentrated on monastic reform; in Lorraine, where they had
learnt much from Cluny, they went further and were interested in the secular
clergy also. But it was principally the
archbishops, the bishops, and in some
cases the lay rulers, who directed the new
movement. The reformers concentrated
on the two principal evils of simony and
clerical marriage, and on some of the
abuses that resulted from lay patronage,
especially over the smaller benefices,
such as the holding of tithes by the laity.
And naturally they tended to magnify the
episcopal office and its importance, while
at the same time they do not seem to have
attempted to interfere with royal authority in the Church. There was certainly no
objection raised to the part played by certain kings, such as Henry II and Henry
III of Germany; on the contrary, it
seemed as natural as it had been in the
days of Charlemagne. The cause of reform was especially furthered when the
kings were favourable; in fact, only when
they were favourable could it make any
real progress.

Among the lay rulers who played a part
in this work were the dukes of Normandy.
They had been in close touch especially
with the reformers in Lorraine, which was
later to provide bishops for England also,
and they had zealously promoted reform
in their duchy. A feature here as elsewhere was the foundation of monasteries;
the monastic life had always been the
ideal, and especially when the laxity of
the secular clergy was so difficult to over-
come. At the same time the dukes maintained an unchallenged authority over
the Church in their duchy. Duke William
acted as his predecessors had done. He
was equally zealous, and quite sincerely

so, as a reformer, and he was more definitely the master of the Church in his
duchy. Not only, as Mr Corbett says, did
he "nominate all the Norman bishops and
invest them with their privileges, but he
was regularly present at the meetings of
Church councils and no ecclesiastical decrees were issued without his sanction."
He was withal zealous for good order and
good government in the Church. He did
not abuse his authority, like his son
Rufus, and above all his appointments
were usually made in the spiritual interests of the Church. His standpoint was
exactly the same as that of Henry II and
Henry III of Germany, and there is no
doubt that it was quite in keeping with the
ideas of the reformers as a whole during
the first half of the eleventh century. It
was in this spirit that he took in hand the
management and the reform of the English Church after the Conquest of 1066.

But already, twenty years before that
date, reform had reached the Roman
Church. By reforming the Papacy, and by
nominating as Popes a series of German
bishops all zealous for reform, Henry III
restored to the Papacy its prestige and
gave to the reform movement its natural
leader. It was particularly the work of Leo
IX that ensured that this should be permanent. Surrounding himself with cardinals of the same mind as himself, drawn
especially from Lorraine, he made certain
of the continuity of policy in the Roman
Church; and by his progress north of the
Alps, in France and Germany, as well as
in Italy, he gave a reality to papal authority which had long been lacking, and attracted popular enthusiasm to his banner.
From this time a new spirit enters into the
Church. There is soon seen to be a cleav-
age in the ranks of the reformers. The old
movement goes on, but the new movement under papal headship, in which the
Church by itself sets its house in order, be-

gins to get the upper hand and to supersede the old. The laity are still encouraged, to help; but they are to be assistants and not directors. Moreover, as many of them do not assist, but even actively oppose reform, the movement tends to concentrate against that lay control of the Church which is often the chief bar to the success of the reformers. With Henry III and with William I cordial relations could still be maintained, but in view of the continual prevalence of simony elsewhere (and simony implies the participation of laymen) the more ardent reformers were clamouring for the removal of lay patronage and lay control of the Church.

This takes some time before it comes to the front. Coincidently, and consequently, was gradually being created the centralisation of the Church under papal headship. The death of Henry II in 1056 removed the chief bar to papal independence, which was given a legal basis in the Election Decree of 1059. The inability of the imperial court to interfere allowed the process to continue unchecked, until with the accession of Gregory VII in 1073 it gathered momentum, and in spite of deadly contest with the ruler of the Empire eventually reached its appointed end. The early stages of the process are all dictated by the desire to effect the reform of the Church, which still remains the first object even with Pope Gregory VII. The enforcement of obedience on archbishops and bishops, who must be responsible for executing locally the decrees passed at Rome, is an important stage. To ensure this obedience, the Pope gives to the legates who are sent with his orders the power to act with full authority in his name. Not only must the archbishop obtain his pallium from Rome; he must go himself to Rome to receive it, and visits to Rome are frequently enjoined on the bishops of all countries. The Popes directly interfere,

too, in the affairs of the local churches, great and small. It is a monarchical authority that replaces the former almost feudal headship of the Church. The papal authority becomes a reality, and finds expression in several directions—legal and judicial as well as administrative. The Pope is supreme legislator, not merely an authority on doubtful points, and his decrees are binding on the whole Church. He is supreme judge, to whom not only the greater cases have to be referred. His court is a court of first instance, to which he can summon any offender. It is also a court of appeal, not only for bishops but for any of the clergy; and it is something more than a final court of appeal, for anyone can appeal at any stage, and appeal to Rome interrupts at once the proceedings in a court of first instance. Finally, the Pope is the representative of St Peter with supreme power over the souls of all men, the judge on all moral issues, the interpreter of God's will to man.

Though this is well known, it was necessary to give this brief summary in order to mark the contrast with the old position. While Reform is still the chief object, and papal centralisation only the means, there will be little quarrel with the rulers who direct the cause of reform in their kingdoms. But soon the establishment of the papal authority becomes the chief end, and while reform is still ardently pursued, it is pursued because it is a necessary part of the work to be done by the head of the Church; this makes a considerable difference in papal relations with the lay powers. The English Church starts in 1066 with the view of its master, King William I; it has come by 1215 to the view of its new master, Pope Innocent III.

This novel assertion of papal authority was not likely to pass unchallenged. In the first place, it was naturally resented by the secular authorities. It threatened to undermine the control they exercised over the episcopate, to turn their officials into papal officials, to divert from them the loyalty of some of the greatest land-holders in the country, and finally to introduce a jurisdiction that would run counter to their own. It mattered little whether the ruler himself was in sympathy with reform or not; all were equally affected. But it was not only the secular rulers who disliked the new state of affairs; the bishops, and especially the archbishops, were for the most part thoroughly hostile to it. Their own ecclesiastical importance and authority were diminished by the authority of a dominant Pope. In many ways this became evident. The control and judgment of elections began to pass from the metropolitans to the Pope; bishops obtained confirmation of their elections and sometimes also consecration from the Pope. Still more did they rebel at having to sit at their own provincial council under the presidency of a Roman priest or deacon, who had come as papal legate to instruct them in the ecclesiastical affairs of their provinces or dioceses. And, again, they had to allow the authority of their ecclesiastical courts to be flouted by any clerk who chose to appeal to the spiritual Caesar. They did not yield without a struggle. Siegfried, archbishop of Mainz, who held the greatest ecclesiastical office in Germany, was not equal to his high position but even he could not remain silent; we can still read his rather shrill protest against what he calls the uncanonical action of Pope Alexander II. We have also a letter of a much more strong-minded prelate, archbishop Liemar of Bremen, to a fellow bishop, in which he writes in a tone of real indignation of the peremptory language in which the papal legates had ordered him to hold a synod, and he was one who had zealously promoted reform in his province. These are two examples out of many from Germany; they can be matched elsewhere. The bishops of North Italy and of France were equally hostile. The Pope had usually one answer to these outbursts—and his tone, though sometimes stern, was usually steady and composed; he had the confidence of right on his side. It was to the decrees of the Fathers, to canonical tradition—in a word, to the law of the Church—that he continually referred them. Clearly there was a conflict as to the law and its interpretation, and it soon becomes evident that it was on the law of the Church that the whole issue was to depend. . . .

* * *

I have gone into these details, many of which I have perforce had to take second-hand from M. Fournier, in order to depict the change in the character of Church law that took place during the century and a half from Burchard to Gratian. The difference between them is enormous in outlook: as the centralisation of the Church under papal government has become the prime feature of Church history, so this is mirrored in the law by which the Church is governed; uniformity to Roman practice has become the rule; the reform programme, common to them both, is now directed by the Pope and is subject to a mass of new papal legislation. The change naturally does not receive universal acceptance at once. Where, as in France, papal authority becomes quickly established, the law as recognised in Rome is there recognised as well. On the other hand, the new collections provided one of the chief means by which the Papacy was able to extend its authority. When archbishop Siegfried in 1074 wrote to Gregory VII, complaining of the uncanonical action of his predecessor Alexander II in punishing a bishop of the province of Mainz whose case had not first been brought before the metropolitan and heard by the bishops of his province, he was maintaining a standpoint which Burchard would have championed. "Uncanonical!" says Gregory in his reply. "My brother, we invite you to peruse with us the canonical traditions and the decrees of the holy fathers." Doubtless he had particularly in mind a passage from a letter of Pope Gelasius I. He possibly read it in the *Collection in 74 Titles,* which had extracted it from the False Decretals; henceforward it is one of the regular entries in canonical collections, and finally is incorporated in Gratian's *Decretum.* And just as archbishop Siegfried was crushed and made no further attempt to quote canonical authority against the Pope, so it was with others. At first the acquiescence is sullen and enforced. But this changes later, especially in France and North Italy, to a willing obedience. And I think that part of the explanation, the chief part, lies in the new canonical collections in which the rising generation was being trained. The young students of Church law read that the first duty was obedience to the Pope; the first place was given to papal authority throughout. And the final stage was reached when the multiplicity of collections, mirroring the different views of individuals, yielded to one single collection, universally recognised and mirroring the papal view. It took a hundred years to reach this final development. Acceptance came at an early stage in France. What happened there was to happen, though somewhat later, in England also. It is this fact that I hope to establish in the pages that immediately follow, and to show the same change taking place, in exactly the same way, in the English Church as in the Western Church as a whole.

PAUL JOACHIMSEN (1867–1930) devoted the greater
part of his published works to the Protestant
Reformation and to fifteenth- and sixteenth-century
humanists. He attended the universities of Heidelberg,
Leipzig, and Munich as a student, and much later
became a professor of history at Munich, where he
spent the rest of his life.*

Paul Joachimsen

The Issue of Government:
Conflict of Church and Empire

In the anointing and the coronation
(936), however, Otto I once again revived
Frankish monarchical ideas in the form
which Pippin and his descendants had
given them. In exchanging his Saxon
dress for the Frankish tunic, he became a
Frank. He entered Frankish territory under Frankish law, like every German king
from that time forward, and by having the
dukes perform the court ceremonies at
the coronation-feast in the capacity of the
four great officers of the royal household,
the most powerful of the racial chiefs once
again became a true Carolingian monarch
and once again united the conception of
sovereign authority with the idea of personal service. In exactly the same way

the dynasty of Pippin had had its beginnings.

After Otto's coronation there followed
in 951 the assumption of government in
Lombardy, and in 962 the imperial coronation in Rome. Each one of these acts
shews that Otto was following directly in
the traces of Charles the Great. The German monarchy, in other words, was irrevocably directed along the path of Carolingian theocracy, and from that time
forward—with a single interruption on
the death of Otto III—it was raised higher
and higher until it reached its culmina-
tion in the monarchy of Henry III, in
which the theocracy of Charles the Great
seemed once more to become a reality.

*From Paul Joachimsen, "The Investiture Contest and the German Constitution," translated by G.
Barraclough, in G. Barraclough (ed.), *Mediaeval Germany, 911–1250* (Oxford, Eng.: Basil Blackwell, 1938),
vol. 2, pp. 98–114, 125–129. Footnotes omitted. The footnotes appearing in the original are available in the
original hard-cover edition just cited.

How are we to estimate the importance of this Romano-German empire in the development of the German people? The old controversy about "Italian policy" and its influence on the destinies of Germany, inaugurated some sixty years ago by Sybel and Ficker, has once more been revived in recent years, but, useful as such argument is for emphasizing the epoch-making character of the great turning-points of history, it can lead nowhere, if we base our judgements on possibilities or alternatives which in reality did not exist. And it is certain that there was, at that time, no possibility of a German federal constitution as an alternative to the imperial structure built up by Otto the Great and his successors; for the two essentials of federal cohesion were lacking. Not only was there no geographical centre within easy reach of all the inhabitants of this huge conglomeration of territories, but Germany also lacked anything which might be considered a spiritual centre, and this was a want which could only have been supplied by a central shrine, such as certain Germanic tribal groups had possessed in heathen times. On the other hand, there was just as certainly no possibility of a German monarchy after the manner of the primitive Germanic "folk" monarchies; for here what was lacking was a sense of German nationality which overrode all tribal divisions. Instead of a German folk there were simply the "tribes" or "stems," in which the dukes had taken the place of the ancient Germanic popular kings. And over the "stem duchies" there was, and could be, nothing except the conception of monarchy handed down from the Franks.

This conception, however, was clerical and theocratic. Not merely because the clergy had preserved it and handed it on as a legacy to the German rulers, but also because the clergy alone offered the monarchy a means of organizing its government. Under both the Ottonian and the Salian dynasties, right down to the beginning of the Investiture Contest, Germany was ruled through the church alone.

Recent studies have done much to clarify the fundamental conceptions on which the relations of the German rulers of this period with the national church rested. The authority which the German ruler exercised over the German church, it has been shown, was the authority of a protector. It was a form of *mundeburdium* [protectorship]—a type of authority as effective in public as in family relationships — and its essential characteristic was the power to represent those who were themselves either completely or partially without legal rights or without an independent legal standing. The German king's position as supreme "advocate" over both the national church as a whole and over individual churches rested on this protective power, with which the "immunity"—an institution of Roman origin— was merged. But the king's position as supreme advocate had an even broader foundation in the Germanic system of "proprietary churches," for on this foundation the idea of the paramount proprietorship of the state over all property in the hands of the national church was built up. Because of this paramount proprietorship the king was entitled to make use of the church and its wealth; and consequently the church provided him with men and accorded him a large part of its income. It is evident that here, as in the development of the mediaeval German constitution as a whole, conceptions of public and of private law were intermingled, and the question whether the public or the private element was predominant is a point which has been widely argued in recent times. In the particular matters which concern us, however, it is safe to say that emphasis of the governmental or public element in the king's position was a legacy from the Frankish period, whereas the powers he possessed as a private person derived from sources common to all primitive Germanic societies. We can say, further, that the conception of public powers, for the very reason that it arose in the closest connexion with the establishment of royal control over the church, will have found expression in both a "realistic" and an "idealistic" form. In the former case, it hardly amounted to more than a justification of the existing constitutional and social order: in the latter, it claimed all the force of a standard of conduct, and its consequences were therefore almost revolutionary.

This difference between a "realistic" and an "idealistic" policy had already served to separate and distinguish the Merovingian from the Carolingian period, and the greatness of Charlemagne is displayed not least by the fact that he was able for a short time to put an end to the antithesis. But it made its appearance again, in the most outstanding way, both as a difference of personality and as a difference of system, in the figures of the first two Salians, Conrad II and Henry III. Of Conrad II's rule Bresslau has written: "Never before and never afterwards, so long as it remained a reality, had the Germano-Roman empire so utterly worldly a character." His son, Henry III, was called by Hauck a model of conscientiousness. And it was this fine, melancholy, lonely man who undertook once again, like Charles the Great, to base his rule on the twin conceptions of *pax* and *iustitia* [peace and justice] in the significance which they had been given in Augustine's *Civitas Dei* [*City of God*].

There is perhaps no better way of approaching the problems which necessarily arose with the transference of the theo-cratic Frankish monarchy into a German environment, than through a consideration of the concepts of *pax* and *iustitia*. When German people spoke of peace and law in the middle ages, they meant by peace either the tribal peace of a primitive age or the king's peace which had developed from it, and thereby they understood the special guarantee or fencing off of one sphere of social life against misdeeds and offences. Whoever committed such misdeeds placed himself outside the "peace" of the community. In the same way the original significance of compensatory payments was that the evil-doer thereby bought himself back into the peace, and it is comprehensible enough that at least a part of the payment fell to the guardian of the peace, who was later the king. By law, on the other hand, the Germanic peoples meant a right, a claim, or in other words what we to-day should call "subjective rights." When the king at his election undertook to vouchsafe each man his rights, or (as was said later) to maintain every man in his law, both parties understood the term in this subjective sense. Objective law in the middle ages was merely "a complex of infinitely numerous subjective concrete rights." Very different, on the contrary, is the position in regard to the ideas of *pax* and *iustitia*. These were taken over by the church from the realm of classical thought, and were developed from beginnings already apparent in Roman times into fixed moral standards. When Augustine spoke of *pax* and *iustitia*, peace was for him the peace of the Kingdom of God, which excludes war and every form of violence, and justice comprehended the *bonum et aequum* [good and equitable] of Ulpian.

From the very hour of his election Conrad II set special store on being a strict and impartial dispenser of justice, and above all on helping the poor and oppressed to obtain their rights. But he understood justice, law and right in an utterly Germanic sense. He had not the least hesitation in enforcing his own or other's claims—for example, against Adalbert of Kärnten—by every means within his power, until his opponent was wiped out, while he took it absolutely as a matter of course that count Giselbert of Loos, after slaying a certain Wikher, should be able to regain royal favour by the surrender of one of his estates. In the legislation which he promulgated, the most evident feature is the endeavour to fix the "condition" of persons and their appropriate rights and duties. For this very reason he shewed no understanding of the great communal movement which was beginning in his day in Italy. His peace was the old German "king's peace": that is to say, the maintenance of order and the repression of rebels and evil-doers.

Wipo, who praises all this and glorifies Conrad as *pacis ubique dator* [giver of universal peace], nevertheless expresses one further desideratum in his admonitions to Conrad's son, Henry, in whose education he had without doubt played some part. He advises the young king to issue an edict on becoming emperor, obliging the German nobility to send their sons to the schools and to have them trained there in the law; for, he says, the Italians have long studied the law and it has made Rome the mistress of the world. In these words Wipo touched on the real weakness of the German realm under the Ottonians and Salians: it had failed to take over, from the rich Carolingian inheritance, the legislative activity which had marked the work of the Carolingian monarchs. Giesebrecht has emphasized the significance which such legislation, had it been introduced, would have had in stabilising the German constitution, and has shown how it would have influenced German legal development by creating a body of objective law. Nitzsch, on the other hand, whose works have cast so much new light on the history of the Salian period, sees in Wipo's proposal an expression of opposition to the whole outlook of the German lay nobility, which avoided a written law as long as possible and emphasized in the education of its sons those poetic and ethical qualities which meet us in the national epics and in the lawbooks of the Hohenstaufen period. Once again this difference of opinion strikingly reveals the antagonism of the conflicting forces within the German constitution of the period. For the formation of a body of written law in Germany would have altered not only the character of German law but also the very position of the monarchy within the German state.

But Henry III did not take the step which Wipo recommended to him. When we see him administering the law in Germany, his attitude is precisely the same as that of his father, and shews the same unqualified acceptance of Germanic legal conceptions. On the other hand, he was strongly influenced by the conception of peace, and unlike his father, he understood this conception in the full clerical sense. When in 1043 he entered the pulpit at the provincial synod in Constance as (in the words of the St. Gallen Annalist) a *facundus orator* [eloquent orator], preached to the people, forgave all who had trespassed against him, and then urged all present "tum precibus, tum pro potestate" [by his prayers and in consideration of his power] to do likewise—a proceeding which he repeated throughout the kingdom—it is clear that the king, who regarded himself both as holy and as sinful, was using the full force of his profound religious convictions to impose peace on his subjects as a moral duty. Only in this way did he feel he could acquit himself of his duty to himself and to his royal office. He was *sacerdos* and *iudex* [priest and judge], as Alcuin had said of Charles the Great.

His attitude towards the church was similar. His father and his father's predecessor, Henry II, like the Ottos before them, had not hesitated to make use of the church. They had accepted the gifts with which bishops and abbots repaid their election, with the same lack of misgiving which had characterized the Frankish rulers. When Conrad appointed a new bishop of Basel in 1025 after the payment of a huge sum of money, it was represented to him that such an action was simony, according to the new clerical conceptions which were just beginning to make themselves felt. He therefore swore he would no longer accept money for the conferment of bishoprics and abbeys— "in quo voto," says Wipo with a true courtier's diplomacy, "paene bene permansit" [He kept this vow quite well]. But the son kept the father's oath. More than any other temporal ruler Henry III helped to set the new view, that simony was a heresy, on its feet. With the acclamation of the reform party he went to Italy in 1046 in order to reform the papacy, which was itself under suspicion of simony, and the monarchical theocracy reached its highest point when the king forced the three claimants of the papal throne to resign at Sutri and Rome in 1046, and then received the imperial crown from the hands of his own pope, the German bishop Suidger of Bamberg. For Henry had as little misgiving about ruling as about reforming the church. The three German popes who now occupied the see of Peter are witnesses to the fact that the Ottonian national church, working through the empire, had captured the papal throne. When the em-peror appointed Victor II, the last of the German popes, to the duchy of Spoleto and the margravate of Fermo, giving him also the powers of an imperial *missus* [intendant], and when on his deathbed, a year later, he enjoined the pope to protect his five year old son, the relation of the "two swords," as it had been understood throughout the early middle ages from the days of pope Gelasius onwards, received its most perfect expression, and at the same time the theocratic outlook of the Frankish monarchy seemed to have been reaffirmed with new force and solidity.

Not quite twenty years later Gregory VII opened the struggle against the last heir of the Frankish theocracy. The appearance which Germany then presented, in the year 1075, was very different from what it had been on the death of Henry III. All the forces which the first two Salians had ingeniously and laboriously incorporated into the edifice of the state had turned back in the direction of independent development, and new forces had made an appearance—forces which had, indeed, existed previously but merely as factors in the social rather than the political situation, and which in any case had been confined within the limits of single duchies or particular districts. To the fore were the old seats of racial opposition, Lotharingia and Bavaria, and with them a new centre of particularism, Saxony. More important was the increasing opposition of the lay aristocracy; more important still the clerical reaction against the idea of theocracy. This had begun already under Leo IX, the third of the popes appointed by Henry III—a pontiff still apparently in complete agreement with the emperor, but showing nevertheless that unmistakable tendency towards clerical independence which was implicit in the Cluniac reform and still more in its manifestations in Lotharingia. Meagre as our information is, it can perhaps be said of Henry that, the longer he lived, the more acutely he came to realise how critical was the situation in his kingdom. In face of clerical opposition, he seems at least to have wavered, if not to have given way in his policy of direct dominion over the church. Three times he forced the nobles to swear allegiance to his son, and the second time the oath contained the highly suggestive addition: "si rex iustus futurus esset" [if he be a just king]. But the most significant feature of all is his recognition of the fundamental weakness of the German constitution: its lack of fixed revenues, on the one hand, and, on the other hand, the lack of an official class to serve in the imperial administration and in the administration of the royal demesne. These deficiencies, however, were a direct result of the renunciation of the revenues which had hitherto been raised by the disposal of positions in the church—a practice which was now regarded as simony. At the time of Henry III's death, therefore, there were already signs that the old Ottonian system was undermined, and both the strength of the German state and the equilibrium of the whole German constitution were left absolutely dependent on the personality of the ruler.

At this critical juncture there followed the minority of Henry IV, and ten years of regency during which the crisis in the German constitution became ever more imminent. It could only have been prevented by a statesmanlike personality of the first rank or by a firmly established administration, capable of functioning by itself. The one came to the rescue of France, the other to that of England, when similar or even more serious difficulties arose; but in eleventh-century Germany both were lacking. The empress Agnes, who took over the government, was anything but a regent of first-rate qualities, such as the great empresses of the Saxon dynasty, Adelheid or Theophano. She had grown up in Aquitanian piety and aspired to the cloister. And yet she did nothing in the years of her regency which Henry III himself might not have done. If she silenced opposition in Lorraine by considerable concessions to the house of Ardenne and the counts of Flanders, it is possible that she was only carrying out Henry's testamentary dispositions. If she once again placed the duchies of Bavaria, Swabia and Carinthia in the hands of feudatories, she was only returning to the position of the early years of Henry's reign; for she could not guess that in the three new dukes, Otto of Nordheim, Rudolf of Rheinfelden and Berthold of Zähringen, she was helping three future enemies of her son to seat themselves firmly in the saddle. And if, probably at the very beginning of her regency, she made the princes swear that, in the event of the early death of her son, they would do nothing to fill the throne without her consent, her object was probably simply to safeguard her son, and so her action falls into line with Henry III's earlier proceedings, when he sought a threefold assurance of his son's succession. But the abduction of the young Henry at St. Suitbertswert in 1062 suddenly threw a vivid light on the political situation. There was no resistance from the empress, and none from princes or people; and, more ominous still, no representative of the national church was found, who would maintain, like the great bishops of the Carolingian epoch, the dignity of the crown. Anno of Cologne and his successors in the control of the young king were egoists, intent on territorial expansion either by increasing their spiritual or by extending their secular authority; and for all of them the royal child was simply an instrument for furthering their personal ambitions.

This development was the more ominous, in so far as these very years saw the final emancipation of the Roman church from imperial and German influence. Under Nicholas II (1058–1061) the papacy drew up a new electoral procedure, which, although intended in the first place only to secure the independence of papal elections from the influence of Roman aristocratic factions, also undermined the position of the German king. Through the Norman alliance it acquired a political counterpoise to German military power, and the popular movement of the Pataria in Milan provided a social counterpoise to the powerful episcopal churches of Lombardy. And finally it obtained a programme of reform in cardinal Humbert of Silva Candida's treatise *adversus Simoniacos* [*Against Simoniacs*], which in pronouncing every grant of an ecclesiastical office by the laity or to the laity to be simony, declared war both on the theory and on the practice of the Ottonian and the Salian monarchy. If there was resistance to these tendencies at the German court, it is noteworthy that it originated no longer in the German church, but with the "rectores aulae regiae" [administrators of the royal court] or "aulici administratores" [court administrators], a group only known to us from the remarks of opponents and therefore difficult to define as regards either composition or activity, but it is clear that the group was not strong enough to support the Lombard bishops in their resistance to the papacy. On the contrary, the papacy made still further progress during the pontificate of Alexander II

(1061–1073), and already there appeared in the background, as the guiding spirit, the monk Hildebrand, who had once accompanied Gregory VI into exile in Germany, and had perhaps imbibed in German reform circles the very ideas which made him a radical opponent of Frankish theocracy.

Such was the situation in 1065, when Henry IV attained his majority and then, a year later—robbed of his adviser, Adalbert, by the jealousy of the princes—began his personal rule. His character has been so distorted by partisan statements that we can no longer delineate it with absolute certainty. But it is at once evident that he was a man who came early to maturity and was endowed throughout his life with extraordinary talents. The violent changes in his upbringing and the humiliations which he then suffered, no doubt taught him to don the "courtier's cloak of invisibility," which was to serve him well on more than one occasion in his later life; but he brought with him to the throne the firm will of a ruler—a ruler, it may be added, less of his father's build than like his grandfather, Conrad II.

Karl Wilhelm Nitzsch to whom we owe not only the most remarkable but also—even in its errors—the most instructive history of the Salian period, described Henry IV's place in German constitutional development in these terms: "he began his reign as a revolutionary, attacking the old constitution: he finished as its last and almost its sole defender." The revolutionising of the old constitution is seen by Nitzsch in Henry's attempts to create in the Harz a permanent centre for his government. From this centre he hoped to use the resources of the silver mines at Goslar; to bring the Saxons into subjection by building castles manned by Swabian *ministeriales* [at this time, serfs in important administrative posts]; and finally to increase the immediate demesne of the monarchy by a general resumption of crown lands. "Henry's early plans for the establishment of a stronger monarchy," says Nitzsch in another place, "would almost certainly have been accepted throughout Germany, if they could have been brought to a successful conclusion at the beginning of his reign. In that case," he continues, "continental Saxony would have been defeated in the same decade in which the Normans conquered the insular Saxons in England; and from that time, without doubt, we should also date the beginnings of an improved governmental organisation in Germany and a new concentration of German national powers, instead of their decline and transformation." It is, of course, another question whether Henry really pursued so conscious and systematic a policy, and what his final objects were. About questions such as this argument will always, in our present state of knowledge, be possible; and any judgement will, in the last analysis, depend on acceptance or rejection of Nitzsch's views. Nitzsch, we have seen, regarded Henry's policy as revolutionary: for Hampe, on the other hand, it was reactionary and directed solely to restoring the ancient rights of the crown. Yet Hampe himself drew attention to the analogy of the French monarchy, which built up its power from its base in the Ile de France; and Henry IV's object was precisely the creation of another Ile de France in what was later to be the very heart of Germany, though in this case it was not built out of the old hereditary demesnes of the royal family, but was the beginning of a new crown territory in the colonized lands. The position was no different at a later date when the Hohenstaufen linked up their castles and demesnes in a continuous chain from Alsace to the Egerland, and then, not content with this, reached out to Lombardy, Tuscany and finally Sicily, or when the Habsburg and Luxemburg dynasties moved the centre of their power from western Germany to the colonial lands of the east. In each case the basic cause was the same: the poverty of the crown demesnes and the endeavour of the monarchy to provide itself with a ministerial personnel and with a permanent revenue. This presupposes that the Ottonian constitution no longer satisfied either of these needs, but it presupposes also that there was in existence a group which regarded the satisfaction of these needs by new methods as possible. Such a group we have every reason, with Nitzsch, to see in the *ministeriales* [serf-administrators]. They are possibly the same class as the *aulici administratores* [administrators at the royal court] who had loomed so large during the regency of Agnes, and are certainly identical with the *familiares* [companions] and *vilissimi homines* [basest men] mentioned by Lambert of Hersfeld, of whose influence over Henry our authorities complain. They began at this period to play a major rôle in the development of the German state, and were destined to become a decisive factor under the Hohenstaufen.

This first attempt of the German monarchy to stabilize its position, both territorially and economically, only became a really important factor in determining the actual course of constitutional development when it came face to face with the opposition of the Saxon folk—the race which, above all others, still embodied the old Germanic spirit of freedom and kept alive the Germanic conception of law. Incidental though it may be, it is very characteristic of the profound antitheses which were at play that the crown under Henry IV set out to recover its actual or supposed rights through the procedure of the Frankish inquisition, while the Saxons countered royal claims by their own ancient law of possession, the basis of which was seisin witnessed by the community.

But the Saxons soon broadened the basis of their opposition. The revolt with which they replied in 1073 to the crown's threats of confiscation, brought into prominence, for the first time in German history, the problem of the ancient Germanic *Widerstandsrecht* [right of resistance], the question of the right to rebel and of legitimate resistance not merely to a particular ruler but also to the crown as such. The significance of this legal concept in the constitutional development of western Europe has recently been brilliantly explained by Fritz Kern. In Saxony the immediate basis of the right to rebel was that specifically Germanic conception of right which we have discussed above—the view that a right is a claim which is established either by the good-faith of the claimant alone or by witnesses and the general belief of the neighbourhood. A conviction of the legitimacy of their cause was therefore regarded as in itself an ample justification for the Saxon revolt, which was simply lawful or even necessary self-help against wrong. The first object of the Saxons was to regain their ancient rights; and whether they hoped to attain other objects by their rising, whether in particular they had already conceived the idea of deposing Henry, are questions which remain uncertain in our present state of knowledge. For we, like the contemporaries who recorded the events, can only see the Saxon revolt through the medium of the greater struggle with which it was so inextricably bound up: the Investiture Contest. At the very moment when Henry had defeated the Saxons and forced them to come to terms, he found himself face to face with a mightier adversary still, the papacy of Gregory VII, which grasped the opportunity to press its demands on the German church and on the German monarchy.

It is not my purpose to argue the question whether or not the German monarchy was forced to regard such demands at such a time as a declaration of war. That it was possible to come to an understanding on the question of investiture, even with a papacy imbued with Gregorian ideas, was proved by the outcome of the contest. That Gregory, even in 1075, was seeking some such understanding is at least likely. It is possible to conceive of an arrangement by which the German crown, its power based on its newly-acquired demesnes which could be converted to the uses of a money economy, and on the energies of the *ministeriales* and of the urban classes in the towns of the Rhineland, who were just entering into the political field, might have played the part assigned to it in Gregory's wide-reaching programme of world-policy: the German king, in other words, acting as advocate and protector of the church in Germany and Italy, while the pope led the church's *militia* to the Holy Land. If such a plan were to be realized, however, it would have been necessary for Henry to put himself at the pope's disposal in purging the German church of simoniacs and incontinent clerks; he would have had to abandon the Lombard church politically and the German church at least administratively and probably also financially. If he perhaps considered this possibility for a moment, there were no tangible results. Exalted by his success in Saxony, he once again united his cause with that of the German bishops, whom Gregory was threatening, and took up arms in defence of his position in Lombardy. When, on 8 December, 1075, Gregory threatened him with the fate of Saul, he opened the struggle by assembling the German episcopacy at the synod of Worms on 27 January 1076. Then follow like the blows of a sledgehammer the great manifestos of the two parties: at Worms, the deposition of Gregory or rather the declaration by the king in his capacity as *patricius urbis Romanae* [patrician of the Roman City] and by the assembled bishops that Gregory's election was invalid; at the Lenten synod in Rome the pope's reply, the suspension of Henry from government and his excommunication; then the king's attempt to reply to this excommunication with the excommunication of the pope in an assembly of German bishops held at Mainz on the feast of St. Peter and St. Paul; next the first defections of German clergy and laity from Henry, the junction of the south German and Saxon oppositions and the forging of a connexion between both and the papacy; the arrangements between Henry and the German princes at Tribur and Oppenheim in October, by which the king was enjoined to free himself from excommunication within four months if he wished to keep the crown; Henry's journey to Canossa and success in obtaining absolution; and finally the election of Rudolf of Swabia as anti-king at Forchheim on 15 March, 1077. Within this circle of incidents are enclosed the events which irrevocably altered the constitution of Germany for its entire future. . . .

The issue is not merely that the German monarchy now becomes for the first time a purely elective monarchy, and that this, in the view of the electors, is to remain a basic principle of the constitution. What is at issue is rather the whole conception of what constitutes the realm. . . .

The combination of Germanic and ecclesiastical ideas had already played some part in Henry IV's deposition by the princes. As the pope, to their astonishment, had kept strictly to the path indicated in his manifesto of 3 September, and had set justice above all else, the princes made good the lack of ecclesiastical grounds for attacking Henry by drawing up a list of the wrongs which they had severally suffered at his hands. Henry was no longer their king, because he had assailed the concrete rights of individuals. For he had been king over each individual, bound separately to each as each was bound to him by the bond of fealty, and the breach of this bond was itself a sufficient justification for resistance. In the minds of those whose opinions Bruno airs, Rudolf of Rheinfelden was again to be such a king. Before his election he was to confirm or restore each individual's rights. Without doubt it was the lay princes and secular magnates who forced this consideration into the forefront of the electoral negotiations; and foremost among them were the Saxons who had already declared at the elections both of Henry II and of Conrad II that the elected king would only become their king after he had confirmed their rights. But in 1077 they deferred to the views of the papal legate, and changed their attitude, merely asking for an undertaking that Rudolf would be a just king. Such an undertaking might appear at first glance to be no more than a return to the ancient formula in the oath sworn by German kings at their coronation, or more specifically to the oath of 1053. And yet it was more than a return to the old order. Rudolf's oath in 1077 was not merely an assurance granted by the elected ruler because of his consciousness of his royal duties: instead, it was the condition under which he received his authority from the electors. Twenty-nine years later the archbishop of Mainz declared this without ambiguity, when he handed over the imperial insignia to Henry V. And the undertaking itself, which was now an essential condition of election, was no longer merely an engagement to a number of individuals, but was rather a pact with an *universitas* [general body]—an *universitas* which represented the realm, just as the realm was now represented by the princes. Such a development followed unmistakably the lines of ecclesiastical thought as laid down by Gregory VII. Gregory's famous letter of 3 September 1076, therefore, does not merely foreshadow the earliest electoral capitulation agreed to by a German king—which was one main innovation introduced by Rudolf's election—but it also contains the germ of the idea that the princes as a body constitute the realm. This conception was the basis of Gregory's attack on the hereditary rights of the monarch; and although it may be said that, for the pope, it was only a subsidiary theory which he adopted in order to secure a victory for the even more far-reaching ecclesiastical principle of *idoneitas* [worthiness] in the ruler, there is no denying the fact that his conception of the realm was definitely a conception of the realm as an *universitas* of the princes. For the future development of the German constitution, however, this latter idea was even more important than the electoral principles enunciated by the pope. The view that the German kingdom was an elective monarchy did not become finally prevalent until some two centuries after the election of Rudolf of Rheinfelden; for Henry IV's struggles against the electoral principle were not in vain. He handed on the ancient theory of hereditary monarchy as an inheritance to his son, and the Hohenstaufen took it over from Henry V and defended it with new weapons. The principle that the princes constitute the realm was, on the other hand, the immediate and permanent result of the Investiture Contest. In their corporate capacity as the realm they ranged themselves between Henry V and the pope, and finally brought about the compromise between the two contending parties which is known as the Concordat of Worms.

The development of the conception of a kingdom represented by the princes was inevitable. The ancient Germanic theory of the state, from which both the Germanic duty of fealty and the Germanic right of lawful resistance were derived, had its roots in a primitive conception of law and an equally primitive conception of the constitution, both of which have been very improperly idealized. It was as necessary to supersede such primitive ideas as it was necessary to supersede the Germanic law of the proprietary church, in which churches were treated simply as material objects. In this connexion it is not without significance to recall the fact that the papal legates at Forchheim compared the Germanic conception of law, as expressed in the demands of Otto of Nordheim's party, with simony. Just as it was impossible for the latter to persist unchallenged in the face of a more informed understanding of the meaning of the church, so also it was impossible for the former to persist in the face of a more advanced conception of the state. Nor was it a misfortune that this new theory of the state was established in direct opposition to the older authoritarian principles maintained by the Frankish monarchy. Exactly the same clash of principles led to the growth of the constitution both in France and in England, and subsequent developments in Germany under the Hohenstaufen shew that, even in the twelfth century, there was still a possibility of reducing the relationship of ruler and realm to the concrete form of a coherent, organic association, such as was gradually established in the feudal states of western Europe. If the assembly at Forchheim, far from beginning a new phase of constitutional reorganisation in Germany, proved in the light of later developments to be the first germ of disintegration, it was because of the failure to replace the seigniorial connexion between crown and people, which had been so magnificently established by Frankish theocracy, by a new corporate association of a governmental character. Otto Gierke has shown us how important a part the corporate association has played throughout the course of German history; but however powerfully it may have affected the social life of the whole community or the political life of smaller units, it proved incapable of creating in mediaeval Germany a general German consciousness of a German state based on the feeling of common responsibility for rights and duties. The political education of the German people, leading to the realization that the German empire, if it is to be a true German state, must be based on such a corporate conception of rights and duties, has been both slow and painful. Even to-day, perhaps it is not quite complete.

DEMETRIUS B. ZEMA (1886–1948) entered the Society of Jesus in London (1912) and studied in the Jesuit Clericate in Holland and at Woodstock College. He was ordained priest at Valkenburg (1923). He joined the history department at Fordham University and served as its chairman (1925–1936). For three years (1936–1939), he had the good fortune to do research in medieval history at Cambridge University as a student of Z. N. Brooke (above, p. 6) and in the Vatican archives. When he returned to Fordham, he became professor of medieval history. The essay here reprinted grew out of Father Zema's archival work, and out of the natural interest he took in Calabria, his native land. Notice especially his emphasis on the economic distress of the papacy as a vulnerable point in the reform movement. He treated the papacy's own measures to remedy this weakness in another article to which reference should be made: "Economic Reorganization of the Roman See During the Gregorian Reform," *Studi Gregoriani*, I (1947), pp. 137–168.*

Demetrius B. Zema

The Issue of Property:
Difficulties Within the Roman See

In the entire course of the Middle Ages no movement surpasses, in enduring importance and absorbing interest, that known as the Gregorian Reform, or, less correctly, the War of Investitures. It is the movement that had its most determined leader in Pope Gregory VII.

After a long period of paralyzing subservience, the papacy, in the line of Pontiffs that began with Leo IX (1048–1054), arose like a giant refreshed and put forth that resolute and long-sustained effort which at length shook the Church free from the grip of secular control, stemmed the tide of corruption that had deranged her normal life and discipline, and, in the end, recovered for itself the effective leadership of the body Christian in Western Europe.

That achievement, though as yet incomplete, was a fact of the first order in the social progress of Europe. And historians who have well gauged the directions of the currents that agitated life in the eleventh century, have also recognized its vast significance. They have at least recognized that in a society still half-developed and still largely addicted to barbarian habits, no other civilizing influence could have set bounds to the tyranny of princes and petty barons, or curbed violence and passion in a feudally

---

*Demetrius B. Zema, S. J., "The Houses of Tuscany and of Pierleone in the Crisis of Rome in the Eleventh Century," *Traditio*, II (1944), 155–175. Footnotes omitted.

decentralized world, than the power which alone represented a long tradition of law and social unity, and alone wielded a universal spiritual jurisdiction over them all. The triumph of the papacy was, in fact, the triumph of the *ordo Romanus* [Roman order] over Germanic particularism, and every agency that contributed to the restoration of that order assumes an historical importance proportionate with it.

But the task of restoration was a tremendously complicated one and so beset with obstacles of a material order, that before the reformers could achieve a fair measure of success, they had to lay their hand to more than purely spiritual instruments. Not least among the obstructions that balked the work of reform, was the widespread alienation and distraint of the Church's temporal resources. For several centuries before the eleventh, the proprietary-church system, so ably brought to light by Ulrich Stutz, had already taken deep root throughout Western Europe; and the effect of its operation was to deliver the majority of parish churches, as well as scores of bishoprics and abbeys, into the private ownership of secular lords innumerable who exploited them as chattel and employed their revenues for personal and profane ends, instead of the religious and charitable purposes for which the ancient canons destined them.

Furthermore, the economics of the Roman See itself had fallen into utter chaos and were well-nigh exhausted. Its landed patrimonies in South Italy and beyond, so productive in the days of Gregory the Great, had long been lost to invaders, and those that remained within the Papal State had for the most part been appropriated by the Roman barons; while an empty treasury is all that the preceding generation of Popes had bequeathed to the reformers. So that, while these were all absorbed in the laborious task of running simony, clerical incontinence and lay-investiture to earth, they were, at the same time, compelled to grapple with the added problem of retrieving lost properties and of seeking out new sources of revenue. Not otherwise were it possible for them to muster the material forces indispensable for carrying on an effective administration, and for maintaining their seat of authority where it belonged, in the Eternal City itself, against the assaults of the local factionists who, always incited by the powers of anti-reform, spared no effort to drive the advocates of the Gregorian plan out of Rome.

It lies beyond the scope of this article to examine that entire phase of the reform struggle which was directed toward the economic recovery of the Roman See and of its religious institutions abroad. No more is intended here than to present, in the light of available sources, a summary account of the part played by two notable families, who coming forward as staunch auxiliaries in a desperate situation, most decisively enabled the papacy to hold Rome and thus continue the fight for reform to a successful issue. Those staunch allies were the house of Tuscany and the family of Pierleone.

I. The House of Tuscany

When we speak of Tuscany in connection with the Gregorian reform, there naturally come to mind the two illustrious women: Countess Beatrice and her more celebrated daughter Matilda. To these, his wife and daughter, Boniface of Canossa, dying in May 1052, left a vast inheritance of feudal and allodial domains that spread from the valley of the Po southward across the Apennines into the valley of the Arno and, beyond that, to the very confines of the Pontifical States.

In the eyes of contemporary chroniclers, the wealth and power of the lords of Canossa were almost fabulous. To build them up, both Church and Empire had contributed their share. Boniface's grandfather, Adalbert-Azzo (d. 988), founder of Canossa, and his father Tedald (d. 1012–1017), had served the Emperor well and from him had received the counties of Reggio, Modena, Mantua and Brescia-Verona as fiefs. From the Pope, Tedald had acquired the county of Ferrara; and, when Boniface himself was created Margrave of Tuscany by Emperor Conrad II, in 1027, he became the richest landlord and the chief feudatory on the Empire in Italy.

Numerous also were the fiefs held of bishoprics and abbeys; and still more numerous the estates acquired in freehold through the process of purchase, exchange, or sheer unsurpation, particularly during the forty years of Boniface's rather notorious regime. Beyond the Alps, in Upper and Lower Lorraine, lay the allodial heritages that fell to both Beatrice and Matilda by reason of their family connections with the ducal house of Lotharingia.

But while the lords of Canossa owed their feudal holdings to imperial favor, it must be pointed out that their private possessions were primarily built up at the expense of the Church. Few indeed, if any, were the bishoprics, abbeys and canonries whose patrimonies, tithes and churches had not been diminished as a result of those spoliative exchanges and libellary contracts which the reformers so strongly reprobated. Even a cursory glance at Falce's *Regesto* of Boniface's acts will reveal how, in most cases, the many exchanges and emphyteutic pacts the margrave made with the churches, were advantageous to none but himself. These facts must be kept in mind if we would see Countess Matilda's subsequent generosity to the religious institutions of her domains in a fuller light.

In 1054, Boniface's widow Beatrice entered into a second marriage with her cousin Godfrey, duke of Upper Lorraine, who thereby became also margrave of Tuscany. But this was done without the Emperor's knowledge and consent and, to aggravate matters for Godfrey, he was then an open rebel of the Empire. On the part of a vassal all this was irregular conduct which no suzerain could overlook. Accordingly, Henry III marched down into Tuscany the following year to bring his vassal to book; but Godfrey fled back to Lorraine to stir up further trouble there, and Beatrice remaining behind was taken to Germany under imperial custody with the then eight years old Matilda. However, before the Emperor died, in October 1056, a sort of reconciliation was patched up, Godfrey was reinvested with the fief of Upper Lorraine, and, in the Spring of 1057, the three were back in Tuscany. But unpleasant memories lingered and by this time had definitely broken the tradition of loyalty that had marked the relations between the house of Canossa and the Empire for so long—a tradition already shaken in the last three years of Margrave Boniface. For the next sixty years Tuscany will be unreservedly ranged on the side of the reform papacy.

Into the politics of the whole situation we need not enter. But for the sake of chronological perspective, we may note that Godfrey passed away at the end of 1069, again leaving two women to govern the margravate. In the same year, too, Matilda, now twenty-three years of age, took to husband her step-brother Godfrey, the elder Godfrey's son known as the "Hunchback," who thus became duke of both Lorraines as well as margrave of Tuscany. But diplomacy rather than love dictated this marriage. Moreover, Godfrey's German interests ran counter to Matilda's papal interests, and his frequent absences in Lorraine rendered the union all but nominal. Then came death to part them and to place Matilda on a new footing. In the early part of 1076, it removed Beatrice and Godfrey from the scene, leaving Matilda the sole heir and ruler of the entire marquisate of Tuscany and proprietor of the spacious inheritance above described. With all this wealth and power now gathered into her hands, the marchioness declared herself univocally for the defence of Pope Gregory VII and the Church, and to that position she faithfully adhered till her own death in 1115.

It now remains for us to assess the extent of material service which the Tuscan allies placed at the disposal of the Reform Popes, and of their assistance to the Church in general. To aid us in this, the sources of information offer, indeed, meagre statistical figures, but many significant facts. And the most significant of these facts is unquestionably the deep religious spirit that motivated the lives and statesmanship of the two countesses, and their constant and active allegiance to the cause of the reform. This devotion was not entirely shared by Godfrey the Elder, and much less by Godfrey the Younger. But in this matter the women's minds were fully made up and it was their will and policy that prevailed. They identified themselves with the plans of Gregory VII from first to last. They attended in person the Roman synods; were in constant touch with the Roman Pontiffs; promoted the reform in their own territories with zeal, and shaped their policy according to the Roman policy. In a word, the interests and needs of the Roman Church were the interests and needs of the house of Canossa. Before and after the death of Beatrice, Matilda's personal attachment to Pope Gregory is the fact that dominates the relations between the Curia and the Tuscan house, and that devotion was not shaken even when Henry IV put Matilda under the ban of the Empire and reduced her possessions to a few castles.

On the strength of this wide-reaching and underlying fact, one should be able to conclude, *ex hypothesi* [theoretically], that as often as the Roman Curia was hard pressed for assistance, financial or otherwise, in order to hold Rome against revolt or siege and to maintain it as base of operations, both Beatrice and Matilda were at once aware of it and ready to aid in the fullest measure.

But the point of the question is: how far did they do so in fact, and in what ways? As already suggested, the chroniclers marvel at the wealth of Tuscany; they speak of Matilda's constant readiness to render service to the Pope, but are sparing in the mention of specific amounts contributed. Yet, Donizo, the monk of Canossa and Matilda's biographer, who had close-hand knowledge of his heroine, does tell us in his rough hexameters that it was "her wont to send many gifts to the Lateran" for which Pope Gregory blessed her. The mention of the Lateran suggests that these gifts were in the nature of financial aids to the papal treasury. And though Donizo is speaking of the gifts sent to Rome on the particular occasion of anti-pope Wibert's desperate attempt to seize the City with the support of Henry IV's troops in 1082, yet he does not limit them to that one occasion. From what we otherwise know of Matilda's open-handed fidelity to the Holy See, we may well suppose that she frequently sent financial relief, and this, the more certainly, when she does not fail to do so at the moment of her own extreme distress. For, it is precisely in 1082, when most of her vassals had fallen away from her, and when the major part of her lands are in the Emperor's hands, that the Countess had the church of Canossa stripped of its plate, had this melted down to the amount of 700 pounds weight of silver and 9 of gold, and then sent the treasure to Rome for financing the defence of the City against the besieging forces of Henry IV and his pope Wibert. Money, to the amount of 200 Pounds, was also despatched from Canossa, while the abbey of Nonantula was likewise stripped of its precious objects for the relief of Rome.

At this point, it is relevant to observe that in requisitioning the treasures of her churches for the defence of Rome against the German forces, Matilda supplied the very help which the Roman prelates themselves refused to accord to Gregory even at the critical moment when he stood with his back to the wall. With the fall of Rome imminent, a council of cardinals and high clergy met on May 4, 1082, either at Gregory's bidding or on their own initiative, in order to consider the lawfulness of pawning the sacred plate of the Roman churches for the defence of the City. Rigidly adhering to the letter of the law, which forbade the alienation of ecclesiastical property, this council decided against the legality of such a step. Were it not, therefore, for the timely arrival of Matilda's gold and silver and money, Rome might have been irretrievably lost to the party of anti-Reform.

But perhaps the most convincing proof of how fully the great lady of Tuscany had dedicated her resources to the support of the Roman See, is to be seen in the exhaustive donation she made to the Church in c. 1079 and renewed in 1102. By this testamentary act the *carissima et fidelissima beati Petri filia* [dearest and most faithful daughter of St. Peter] made over to the Holy See her entire allodial inheritance in full proprietorship. True enough, during her lifetime Matilda reserved all rights of disposal, even to the

extent of making her kinsman Emperor Henry V, by a transaction that still remains obscure, heir to these rights. But the Church's right of ownership is left intact and it is explicitly reserved in grants made to third parties after 1102. During the reform, however, the donation itself had little income value for the Lateran fisc beyond the annual tribute or census payable in recognition of papal proprietorship by those who had received tenures from Matilda. Few were astonished when at her death, early in July 1115, Henry V, besides the fiefs, claimed all her other property in virtue of the private and obscure pact of 1111. For the rest of the century, the Popes will be engaged in perpetual litigations for its recovery. But in the end, they did retrieve the bulk of it and only then was the Roman Curia able to reap the tangible fruits of Matilda's liberal gift.

And yet, it is also true to say that, even in the lifetime of the "great Countess," the Holy See did indirectly and to a large measure enjoy the economic benefits of the famous donation. For everything points to the general fact that Matilda used and administered her possessions in conformity with ecclesiastical policy and interests. Her charities were never exhausted. Donizo gives us a picture of the Countess's court as a haven of refuge for Reform prelates and clergy who had been despoiled and impoverished in the great conflict, and who from her obtained clothing and other relief and never went away disappointed.

But it is the churches and cloisters of her domains which seem to have been the chief beneficiaries of Matilda's bounties. It has already been suggested that under the rule of her father Boniface the churches of the Tuscan domains were systematically mulcted for the aggrandisement of his house. That course of action is now reversed by Beatrice and Matilda. No longer are bishoprics, abbeys and churches pacted out of their tithes and lands. On the contrary, they are now the recipients of one donation after another. The most striking evidence of this reversal of policy is furnished by a comparison of Margrave Boniface's charters calendared by Falce with those of Beatrice and Matilda calendared by Overmann. In the former, which run from the year 1030 to the year 1052, one will note with interest that contracts of emphyteusis, sale and exchange, in which Boniface gets the big, and the churches the small end of the bargain, distinctly predominate. Typical of such jobbery is the exchange transaction with the Canons of Parma, on February 18, 1039, whereby Boniface relinquishes 800 *jugera* of land but receives no less than 1900 in return. But not one of such extortionate deals is recorded in Matilda's regests. What we read there instead, is an almost unbroken series of donations, confirmations, judgments and vindications, all in favor of religious establishments. These constitute 109 out of the 147 acts of the two countesses calendared from 1046 to 1115. Of alienations, the only recorded instances occur when Matilda requisitioned the precious plate of St. Apollonius of Canossa and that of Nonantula for the relief of Gregory VII in 1082. But both of these holy places received subsequent compensation for their losses.

It is true that before her first donation to the Church, in 1079, Matilda did not relinquish the proprietorship of her bishoprics and abbeys, nor the right to dispose of them after that event. Moreover, in view of the extortions of her predecessors, Matilda's bounties to the churches must assume the aspect of a restitution. The fact is, however, that both Beatrice and Matilda placed the religious institutions of their domains on a sound economic basis

and tolerated in them none but Reform prelates and discipline. In so doing they admirably served the ends of the Reform and achieved the very purposes which Gregory VII was striving against great odds to realize elsewhere.

But the material assistance which the rulers of Tuscany gave to the Church went beyond money subsidies to the Curia and donations to the churches of their domain. Of incalculable value was also the military support they afforded to the hard driven Popes. To furnish all the troops needed in order to seat and keep the lawfully elected Pontiffs in secure possession of the Roman See against the forces that opposed them, papal resources, both military and financial, were utterly inadequate. Of pontifical troops, the Lateran fisc could only maintain a body so small that it had to be reinforced from without at every crisis; and recurring crises in Rome were typical of the whole Reform period. Every Pope of the Reform party had, for shorter space or longer, to hold Rome against a rival or abandon it altogether until he could fight his way back into the Leonine City or the Lateran. Thus, Nicholas II had to contend with John of Velletri; Alexander II with Cadalus of Parma; Gregory VII, Victor III and Urban II with Wibert of Ravenna; and Paschal II with the three intruders Theodoric, Albert and Maginolf. In all these cases, the Reform Pope had to outmanoeuvre his adversary with armed force and outbid him with distributions of money, in order to secure both the armed support and the favor of the Roman people. The anti-popes were, therefore, the most dangerous obstacle to the progress of reform—an obstacle that could not have been removed without troops and money. In these crises the Norman vassals also sent troops and money, but never so faithfully and regularly as did the ladies of

Canossa. Indeed, more than once the vassals of the south defaulted and even turned their arms against their suzerain the Pope, but an army from Tuscany was always there to protect him both from the forces of the anti-popes and, at times, from the Normans themselves.

Thus, in 1059, Beatrice's and Godfrey's troops escorted Pope Nicholas II safely to Rome and obliged the anti-pope Benedict X to withdraw. Similarly, in 1061, they furnished defence for Pope Alexander II and for three years counterchecked the movements of the usurper Cadalus who, provided with money and soldiers by the Lombard bishops, vainly strove to take possession of the City. In 1066, they drove the Pope's own refractory vassal, Richard Prince of Capua, out of the papal territory he had invaded, and restored the Campagna to the Holy See, after which the Normans renewed their oath of vassalage.

In 1076, there began the bitter contest between King Henry IV and Gregory VII, the initial stages of which were marked by Henry's excommunication, his deposition by the revolting princes at Tribur, and his diplomatic submission at Canossa. Henry's case was to be decided by a council planned at Augsburg for February 1077, and Gregory himself was to preside. He waited for the promised safeconducts and escort that were to see him safely across the Alps, but neither came; for the German princes and Henry, trusting more to the decision of arms than to that of a council, had determined to fight it out. At the same time, the rank and file of Lombard bishops and barons were ranged on Henry's side and bore no kind of good will toward the Reformer. It was a time of no small personal danger for the Pope as he waited in Northern Italy for a favorable moment to cross into Germany; and more than one enemy could have

been found at this time to repeat the assault perpetrated on the person of the Pontiff by one Cencius in Santa Maria Maggiore on the Christmas night of 1075. But at least one powerful ally stood by Gregory during this perilous interval, and it was none other than the *bellipotens* [martial] Matilda. It was she who for the space of more than eight months—from December 1076 to September 1077—gave him vigilant hospitality and military protection in her castles of Lombardy and Tuscany, and finally escorted him back to Rome unharmed.

By March 1080, the breach between Gregory and Henry had become final and complete and from now on it was to be a war without truce. For thwarting the convocation of the Augsburg council, and for all his other "disobediences," Pope Gregory declared Henry excommunicate and deposed, at the Lenten Synod of 1080, and at the same time recognized Rudolf of Suabia as king of Germany. Henry replied at Brixen, in June of the same year, by electing and putting into the field a pope of his own in the person of Wibert, Archbishop of Ravenna, who styled himself Clement III. Then descending into Italy with an army swollen by the contingents of Lombardy, the banned monarch moved on with ultimate intent of seizing Rome and putting the papal government into his protégé's hands. There is no doubt on whose side Matilda stood. She stood on the side of papal authority and this determined her juridical position as against Henry. For in her eyes, the king her cousin was an excommunicated and deposed monarch, no longer the head of the Empire and no longer her suzerain. Whatever troops she could command she now put into the field against Henry, stubbornly checking his progress towards Rome and giving no rest to the imperial forces supporting the anti-pope. In

Henry's eyes, of course, Matilda was a rebel vassal guilty of high treason, and such he solemnly declared her to be, at Lucca in July 1081, when he released her own vassals from their oath of fealty to her and placed her under the ban of the Empire. The king's soldiery wasted her domains and drove her with her reduced support frgm castle to castle. But there was no yielding on Matilda's part. She fought on, and, for the next three years, while German troops beleaguered Gregory VII in the Eternal City, the lady of Canossa even found means of sending the aid of money and treasure to the Pope in his utmost need. And when Henry left Italy, in the summer of 1084, Matilda rallied vassals and fighting men, took the offensive and delivered a smashing defeat to the king's Lombard supporters at Sorbara in the plain of Modena.

After his fateful rescue and the lamentable sack of Rome by Robert Guiscard's Normans, Pope Gregory lingered another year in exile and ended his eventful and stormy pontificate at Salerno, on May 25, 1085. With Henry's partisans in possession of Rome and an anti-pope installed in Saint Peter's, all of Gregory's efforts to secure the liberty and the supremacy of the Apostolic See, and thereby to achieve the Church's reform and freedom from secular control, seemed to have ended in failure. But such was not Matilda's view of the matter.

In Henry's absence from Italy (1084–1090), her position in the North had appreciably improved; but the situation in Rome was nothing but chaotic. The rescue expedition of the Normans had left the region between the Colosseum and St. John Lateran a smouldering waste and the populace seething with bitter resentment; while disorder was further heightened by the presence of the anti-pope, who held points of vantage and had the support of

an army to challenge the entry of a legitimate Pope into the pontifical city. Dispirited by the gloomy outlook, the cardinals had been slow and fearful about proceeding to a new election and had left the papal see vacant for a whole twelvemonth. This situation Gregory had well foreseen. A small Norman garrison had, indeed, been left behind for the moment to guard the Castel Sant'Angelo; but Robert Guiscard himself had followed Pope Gregory to the grave within less than two months, and the discords that ensued in Norman Italy made it plain that no hope could be pinned on effective help coming from that quarter.

At this point Matilda, as if clad with Gregory's mantle, becomes the soul of the reforming party and its most determined champion. Her first task at this juncture was to hasten the election of a Pope. Accordingly, her urgent summons and her assurance of protection went to every prelate within reach, and it was in answer to her instances that they finally met in the deaconry of Santa Lucia in Rome and, in spite of his obstinate and repeated refusals, chose Desiderius, Abbot of Monte Cassino, to succeed Gregory as Victor III. This was on Whitsunday, May 24, 1086.

But the doubts Desiderius entertained about the validity of his election, his unconquerable reluctance to quit the peace of his abbey for the ferment of Rome, and the presence of the imperial anti-pope who made Rome insecure, decided him to flee back to Monte Cassino only four days after his election and to put off his consecration for yet another year. Having at length made acceptance, Desiderius was brought by Norman troops back to Rome for his consecration, which took place at St. Peter's on May 9, 1087. But in a few days he again hastened to the holy mount. Yet, his place was in Rome, and Matilda, whose armed forces aiding the papal militia now held the Leonine City and Traste-vere, urgently pressed him to return to his See. He complied and, thanks to her military escort, Pope Victor regained St. Peter's in early June, entered Rome by Trastevere and took possession of Sant' Angelo and the right bank of the Tiber. But the strain and worry shortened his days, which ended at Monte Cassino four months later, September 16, 1087.

By this time, however, the Wibertines were back in force and had also retaken the Sant'Angelo stronghold. And now, anxious lest a long interregnum give the anti-pope time to consolidate his position in Rome, Matilda again dunned the card-inals with letters and messengers urging them to give the Church a Pope without delay. This they did only on March 12 of the following year, at Terracina, when they made the excellent choice of Eudes, Cardinal-Bishop of Ostia and one of Gregory VII's own designees, who took the name of Urban II. But only by the aid of men-at-arms could the new Pope gain his See.

It was thus that in the last days of June 1089, Urban's militia, unaided by any Norman or other stranger contingent, beat back the anti-pope's forces and en-abled the new Pope to carry through his coronation and inthronization in St. Peter's on July 3. The Wibertines were as yet nested in the strong places of Rome. But with the havoc wrought by Gregory VII's Norman allies still before the eyes of the Romans, Pope Urban thought it wisest to refrain from any further move that might entail bloodshed and arouse the populace against him. He therefore de-cided to suffer the presence of the anti-pope's supporters in the City until a more propitious moment had arrived for their expulsion. Consistently with that, Urban did not beg the aid of Matilda's troops in Rome at this time.

But in her own domains the Countess will have much military service to render against the Pope's enemies during the eleven years of his pontificate. For war clouds were again over Northern Italy where things were not going at all well for Henry IV. There, Matilda remained the centre of resistance to the imperial adversary of the papacy, and in the six years of his absence she had recovered much of her lost territory and prestige. More than that, she had formed an al-liance with Welf, Duke of Bavaria, ce-mented at Pope Urban's instance by her marriage to Welf's young son, Welf V, thereby creating a more powerful support for the Gregorian cause and a more pow-erful opposition against Henry and his schismatic partisans. With so much fat in the fire to claim his attention, the Ger-man king marched through the Brenner Pass down into Italy with as large a force as he could muster, in the Spring of 1090: this time more determined than ever to crush once for all the power of the belli-cose Countess who had so obstinately de-fied him and so doggedly upheld the in-terests of his deposer.

Bent upon this purpose Henry IV spent seven continuous years in Italy. His first blows against Matilda were crushing. Having, after a long siege, taken posses-sion of Mantua, the key to Matilda's States and beaten her forces at Tricontai, Henry swept southward across the Po Valley seizing the Countess's strongholds one af-ter the other. By June 1092, Henry is on the heights dominating Modena, and Ma-tilda, with the remnants of her vassals, at bay on the hills behind Reggio. In the eyes of many of her vassals and of Urban's friends, Matilda's plight was desperate and certain disaster lay ahead. They joined in urging peace, and yielding to their instances she consented to an armis-tice in the summer of 1092, in order to allow parleys in view of a settlement with Henry. But when the king laid down as preliminary condition for peace that Matilda recognize the imperial pope Clement III and repudiate Urban II, parleys went no further. The Countess declared herself irrevocably for the cause of the Reform Pontiff and the order of things for which he stood, and for that she would continue to fight to the end.

By this time, however, Henry must have realized that his quarrel was not with a mere pious devotee of the Roman Popes, but with the *virago* [manlike] and *athleta comitissa* [vigorous countess], the *virilis animi* [virile-souled] and *bellipotens* [martial] woman whom contemporaries described in these terms. For that woman had been educated both by family tradition and by the school of experience not only in the art of government but also in the art of war. She knew strategy and tactics; could ride and wield the battle-axe with skill; she had inherited the martial courage of her father, and, more than all, could inspire and lead men into battle by the force of her personality. This was brought home to the king very soon.

In October 1092, Matilda stood on the heights of Reggio with two fresh garrisons, one poised at Bianello and the other at Canossa. Attempting a deceptive manoeuvre Henry feigned to be moving toward Parma; then, of a sudden, he turned for an attack upon Canossa—the Canossa of bitter memory at whose gates he had stood a drab penitent fifteen winters previous. But Matilda's men had been all eyes. As the Germans drew near the rock, a dense fog arose confusing their vision and movements; whereupon, the Tuscan knights issuing forth from both strongholds, caught the attackers between pincers, captured the imperial standard and forced them to beat a hasty retreat.

It was the turning of the tide which soon overwhelmed Henry. Matilda's archers pursued the retreating imperialists all the way back across the Po recapturing, as they went, all that had been lost in the beginning of the war.

It is not possible here to enter into a description of that series of spectacular battles and tactics by which Matilda's little armies drove the unhappy king out of her province. But for the military historian they would furnish many highly colorful and dramatic chapters. Nor can we enter into the other episodes of this phase of the Investiture Contest, such as the revolt of Henry's son Conrad, Matilda's separation from Welf, the rise of communal government in Northern Italy, etc. But it does pertain to our purpose to note that, thanks to Matilda's military successes, the way to Rome is more than ever barred to Henry; that imperial officers and schismatic bishops are driven out of their posts; that the great cities of the North conclude a twenty-year alliance with Matilda; and that Italian opinion gradually rallies in favor of the Pope leading the Reform.

The clearest proof of this changed situation is that, in the Spring of 1095, while Henry IV has retreated in isolation to Verona, the way is clear and safe for Urban II to come north and to hold at Piacenza, and later at Clermont, the two celebrated councils which mark so triumphant a stage in the progress of the Reform movement. It is at these same councils, it will be recalled, that the papacy is able to summon Christendom to the Crusade, and this so independently of the secular powers, that at the very moment of the summons, the great sovereigns of Europe, Henry IV of Germany, Philip I of France, and William Rufus of England, lie under the ban of excommunication. To be sure, the battle for reform was not yet over, but already the Roman Pontiff, pursuing the policy of Gregory VII, stood out as the veritable head of Christian society, able to call high churchmen and lay princes to duty, as sole defender of Europe against the advance of Islam.

Urban's return from Clermont was a genuine triumph. At the head of her army Matilda accompanied the Pope, in the late Autumn of 1096, the length of her domains to the gates of Rome, and remained to assist at the great council which, in January 1097, Pope Urban celebrated at the Lateran with all freedom and solemnity. The anti-pope Clement III had been compelled to leave Rome as early as the Spring of 1092 never to return, though his partisans within the City gave the papal militia enough to do.

Viewed on its whole terrain, the war for reform was fought with arms on two fronts: the Roman or home front against the anti-popes, and the Lombard and Tuscan front against their German master. On both fronts, and for thirty years, the house of Tuscany fought with constancy and sacrifice. Through all this, the great issue that dominated all others, was whether Christendom was to be led by a Pope who was a German nominee serving imperial interests, or by one who was canonically elected and free to remove those deep-rooted abuses which gangrened Christian life. In view of the material and lay interests long vested in those abuses, and of the violent character of the resistance challenging attempts at reform, that issue was not to be decided by conciliar legislation and by ecclesiastical censures alone. Arms and money were needed, and these the rulers of Tuscany supplied in generous measure. All the facts and evidence warrant the assertion that, in the worst days of the conflict between the Papacy and the Empire, the marquisate of Tuscany, particularly under Matilda's government functioned for all intents and purposes as a papal State,

furnishing the Roman Curia with the men and money it did not itself command in order to hold out against formidable opposition and to sustain the Reform struggle to a fairly successful issue.

II. The House of Pierleone

We must now turn to the Pierleoni. This notable family of Rome emerged into history when a certain wealthy Jew, Baruch, already married to a Christian lady of the house of Frangipane, himself embraced Christianity some ten years before the arrival of Pope Leo IX. At his baptism he took the name of Benedict and was thereafter known as Benedictus Christianus. By the end of 1051, Benedict was dead. He was succeeded by his Christian son Leo who, in a contract of emphyteusis, dated November 1051, with the monastery of Sts. Cosmas and Damian, is described as "vir magnificus et laudabilis negotiator filius Benedicti bone memorie Christiani" [a superb man and an estimable merchant, son of the late Benedictus Christianus]. By 1059, Leo is regarded as one of the most distinguished personages of Rome. In 1060, he witnesses the transfer of the Sabina castles of Tribuco and Arce, claimed by the Crescentii, to the abbey of Farfa, and in 1061 he is numbered among the leading supporters of Alexander II against anti-pope Cadalus. After Leo's death, c. 1063, it is his son Peter who stands prominently at the head of the family for the next sixty years; and from this Peter son of Leo, or Petrus Leonis, the Pierleoni derived their name. Peter's progeny was numerous. No less than nine sons perpetuated and multiplied the branches of his lineage and spread them in all directions. Zazzera derives even the Hapsburg dynasty from the Pierleone stock, though by a questionable genealogy. One of these sons, Petrus Leonis II, climbed to the papal chair as Anacletus II, in 1130, but eight years later had to relinquish it to the more widely supported Innocent II.

Of some interest to us is the genealogical relation of the Pierleoni with Popes Gregory VI and Gregory VII. Looking closely into this matter, both Professor Fedele and Dr. Poole think it very probable, as Zazzera before them had thought it certain, that Gregory VI, or John Gratian, was the son of Benedict the Christian and, therefore, a brother of Leo and an uncle of Peter. But while Prof. Fedele ascribes a Jewish origin to Gregory VII, or Hildebrand, by making him out to be the grandson of Leo by a daughter Bertha and, therefore, a nephew of Gregory VI, Dr. Poole can only see in the Pope's mother Bertha a gentile sister of Leo's wife, and in Gregory VII, only a gentile nephew of the same Jewish Leo, and hence no blood kin of Gregory VI. M. Tangl also denies Jewish ancestry to Gregory VII, though not for reasons that appeal to Dr. Poole. From the conclusions reached by the three scholars, it may then be held as almost certain that Gregory VI was a blood relation of the Pierleoni; as strongly probable that Gregory VII was connected with them on the mother's side; but as entirely uncertain that there was any Jewish blood in him, despite his allegedly Semitic looks.

But of more immediate relevance is the fact, upon which all are agreed, that the Pierleoni were a family of extremely wealthy financiers; that John Gratian shared their wealth; that Hildebrand had close ties with John Gratian, his namesake in the papacy; and that he was reputed to have had business relations with the moneyed house, a thing that Hildebrand's function as comptroller of the papal treasury, and provider both for the abbey of St. Paul and the Curia, renders more than likely. But above all these considerations, in point of evidence, is the fact that throughout the Reform contest the Pier-

leoni stood squarely and steadfastly on the side of the Reform Popes, affording them refuge, men and money, and always formed a positive counterweight to the Roman aristocracy and German party in the struggles between Popes and anti-popes that so often divided the apostolic city from 1059 to 1122.

The main quarter of the Pierleoni was the Trastevere region, on the right bank. In the eleventh century, they also commanded the double-bridged island of St. Bartholomew (the *Insula Tiberina* or *Lycaonia*); the Theatre of Marcellus, on the left bank, which they turned into a fortress-tower to guard the approach to the island; and also a strong place at the north-east corner of the Forum, near the Mamertine prison. On this part of Rome the Reform Popes could always fall back to safety as often as they were driven out of the Leonine City or the Lateran.

At the end of the year 1058, when Nicholas II was elected in Siena and escorted to Rome by Hildebrand "cum quingentis equitibus et cum magna pecunia" [with 500 cavalrymen and a large sum of money] furnished by Beatrice of Tuscany, the Roman barons had already won with gold many people to the side of their own nominee, John of Velletri, and were in control of the City. At this emergency, the Pierleoni begin to play their part. They forthwith sent instructions to Hildebrand's party that it was safest to lead the new Pope into Rome by way of Trastevere and the island, and thence to the Lateran. At the same time, Hildebrand also sent money ahead wherewith to wean the people away from the support of the anti-pope. This money was furnished in large measure by Benedict the Christian. With his aid, Nicholas II was able to possess himself of the Lateran and to force the barons' candidate to withdraw from the scene. This achieved, Hildebrand hastened to the South, and in brief space returned with the first Norman reinforcements. It is worth noting how in this event all those auxiliary forces are joined whose combined aid, throughout the Reform conflict, will time and again make up the material deficits of the Roman Curia and finally enable it to win the day for the Gregorian party against all anti-popes. On this particular occasion, there came money and troops from Tuscany, money and troops from the Normans, and money and troops from the Pierleoni.

The operations that brought Nicholas II safely into Rome, to hold there the memorable council which radically reshaped the law of papal elections, are episodes typical of every other papal succession during the Reform period. They will be repeated very soon and at greater length after the election of Nicholas' successor, Alexander II, in 1061. Here again the anti-pope Cadalus gains Rome, this time by aid of the imperial troops in conjunction with the Roman nobles, and seizes St. Peter's and the Castel Sant'Angelo. But once more, the wealthy Jewish friend, now Benedict's son Leo, stands behind Hildebrand resisting and counter-attacking the anti-pope with arms and money. The struggle is bitter, intermittent and prolonged for three years. But Leo, son of Benedict, remains in it with his support until Alexander is acknowledged Pope by Romans and Germans alike, in 1064, and his rival Cadalus must ransom himself out of Rome.

After this, it is Leo's son Peter, the most famous of the Pierleoni, who comes to the fore, and for the next three-score he is the most prominent local magnate sustaining the Reform and the course of papal politics. We have every reason to believe that, after Hildebrand himself became Pope in 1073, Peter Leo continued to aid with his purse and power. Since Peter Leo resided on the very scene, we need not wonder that Gregory's *Registrum* contains no

letters addressed to him. But of uninterrupted financial relations between the Pope and the Pierleone banking house there can be no doubt. In view of Gregory's continued responsibility for providing funds; of the interest in the Church's success on the part of those furnishing the funds; and of the fact that they had already furnished large sums, one can only conclude that much of the Pierleone capital was placed, and most likely invested, in the service of Gregory's cause. This would adequately explain one of the persistent fears that agitated Hildebrand's enemies: his extraordinary power for financing all his projects and resisting those of Henry IV. In all of Benzo's phantastic charges, and in all the aspersions of the anti-Gregorians concerning the Pope's financial dealings, there may be said to be this kernel of truth: that the money of Pierleone, whether by way of gift or by way of banker's loans, was in time of need placed at the Pope's disposal, though our sources mention no specific sums.

And what is true of money is also true of services and armed help. When, during the siege of Rome in the Spring of 1082, the Emperor's forces broke into the Leonine City, resolved to end the whole struggle by seizing the person of Pope Gregory VII, it was under the protection of Pierleone that the Pontiff reached the fortress of Sant'Angelo in safety to remain there till Robert Guiscard rescued him in the ill-fated May-end of 1084.

Under the next two pontificates the Pierleoni are at the forefront of Roman affairs and the chief local protectors of Popes Urban II and Paschal II. Shortly after his consecration in May 1088, Urban was forced out of Rome by the soldiery serving Wibert of Ravenna. He returned in November of the same year, but the imperial pope's party still held the principal places in its hands, and it was only on the island of St. Bartholomew, under

Pierleone's shelter that he could take up an abode. In the following June, the Wibertines were dislodged from their points of vantage, but when King Henry made his last descent into Italy in the Spring of 1090, and Matilda's resources were all engaged in the war of the Po, they rallied again, took possession of Sant'Angelo and obliged Urban to quit Rome, and it was three years before the Pope could regain his episcopal See, and seven before he could recover the Castle. But once again, it was Pierleone who cleared the way for the Pope to return to the City in 1094, and it was Pierleone again to whom the fortress on the Tiber was surrendered on the eve of St. Bartholomew in the August of 1098. It was also in Pierleone's house near the Mamertine, that Urban breathed his last in the midsummer of the following year.

Nor did the lords of Trastevere fail to lend their constant support to Paschal II. So much did the new Pope rely on their fidelity and aid that, during his absence in France in 1107, he delegated to them the government of Rome. They are participants in the recovery of the Ponzia and Affile castles in 1109, and in the pacification of Ninfa in 1110. The year 1111 was a particularly distressing one for Pope Paschal. In its early months, Henry V came to Italy resolved to settle the question of investitures, and to receive the imperial crown entirely on his own terms. The whole story need not be told here; but it is pertinent to mention that, in the negotiations and exchanges of pledges preliminary to the forced treaty of Ponte Mammolo, the Pope's spokesman and bondsman was none other than Pierleone. It was he who assumed responsibility for the king's safe-conduct, who gave hostages from his own family and all required guarantees for the fulfillment of the Pope's part of the pact.

After Countess Matilda's death on the second day of July 1115, Pierleone remained the chief support of the Gregorian party in Rome. To his arms and money Paschal II's successor, Pope Gelasius II, owed his delivery from the hands of the Emperor's confederate, Cencius Frangipane, in 1118, and Pope Calixtus II, the delivery of the Leonine City, in 1120, and his riddance of the anti-pope Burdinus the following year.

But we need not pursue the story of the Pierleoni's alliance with the Holy See any further. Taken together, the facts which have been pointed out amply justify the conclusion that the finances and influence of this convert family contributed to the saving of the Reform in a decisive degree. The fact stands out unmistakable that the money, arms and service they so unfailingly furnished between 1058 and 1122, were effective in turning the tide against every anti-pope that raised his head in Rome during that period. There were, forsooth, also the money and troops of Matilda and of the Normans, and, as often as these worked together, it is difficult to measure exactly the value of each party's contribution. But the circumstance that the Pierleoni were at home in Rome and controlled a strategic portion of the City, as well as the power which money gave, unquestionably enabled these auxiliaries to observe and move against local intrigues, to meet emergencies with more despatch and efficacy than was possible for the more distant Normans, had they the will, and for the hard-pressed Countess of Tuscany. In spite of all temporary setbacks and defeats, the reforming Pontiffs held on to Rome and the papal government, and surmounted all opposition. To what extent they had to thank the Tuscan ladies and the Pierleoni for their success, the facts set forth above should enable us to form a fairly correct judgment.

On the level of theory, the great question that lay under debate between Gregory VII and his enemies was this: Did the Pope's measures restore the rightful order of the Church, which bad practices had interrupted, or did they destroy the order which Holy Scripture sanctioned and the practice of centuries approved? In other words: Did Gregory abolish corruptions and recover tradition, or abolish tradition and introduce an evil and perverse new order? On the answers to this question hinged controversy on other critical issues, such as the proper relations of pope and king, and the authority of the pope within the Church's priestly hierarchy. The following texts give the opposing answers of Gregory VII and Henry IV. Though embedded in the contemporary, official collection of Gregory's letters, the *Dictatus Papae* are probably a list of chapter headings for excerpts of canonistic texts that supported the Pope's position. The other documents were consciously written as propaganda. The views of Gerhart B. Ladner and Karl F. Morrison show how difficult it is to reach a common opinion on the motivations expressed in these documents.

Texts

Gregory VII's Position;
Henry IV's Position

GREGORY VII'S POSITION

Dictatus Papae (1075)[1]

1. That the Roman church was founded by the Lord alone.

2. That only the Roman pontiff is by right called "universal."

3. That he alone can depose or reinstate bishops.

4. That his legate—even if of an inferior rank—takes precedence of all bishops in council; and he can give sentence of deposition against them.

[1] From E. Caspar (ed.), *Das Register Gregors VII* (Berlin, 1920–1923), Reg. II, 55a: pp. 202–208. Translated by Karl F. Morrison.

5. That the pope can depose absentees.

6. That, among other things, we ought not to stay in the same house with persons excommunicated by him.

7. That it is permitted for him alone, according to the need of the time, to establish new laws, to form peoples into new congregations, to make a canonry into an abbacy, and, on the other hand, to divide a rich episcopacy and unite needy ones.

8. That he alone can use imperial insignia.

9. That only the pope's feet are to be kissed by all princes.

10. That his name only is recited in churches.

11. That this is a unique name in the world.

12. That it is licit for him to depose emperors.

13. That it is licit for him to transfer bishops, under pressure of need, from see to see.

14. That he has the power to ordain a cleric from any church to whatever place he wishes.

15. That a man ordained by him can preside over another church, but not do military service; and that he ought not to receive a higher rank from another bishop.

16. That no synod ought to be called "general" without his command.

17. That no chapter or book can be held to be canonical without his authority.

18. That his sentence ought to be reconsidered by no one, and he alone can reconsider [the judgments] of all.

19. That he ought to be judged by no one.

20. That no one may dare condemn a person appealing to the Apostolic See.

21. That greater cases of any church ought to be referred to her [the Apostolic See].

22. That the Roman church has never erred, nor, by Scripture's testimony, will it ever err.

23. That the Roman pontiff, if he be canonically ordained, indubitably becomes holy through the merits of Blessed Peter, according to the witness of St. Ennodius, Bishop of Pavia, with many holy Fathers concurring, as is contained in decrees of Blessed Symmachus, the Pope.

24. That by his precept and license it is licit for subjects to bring charges.

25. That he can, without a synodal assembly, depose and reinstate bishops.

26. That no one is considered catholic who is not in harmony with the Roman church.

27. That he can absolve subjects of wicked men from fealty.

Gregory's Second Letter to Bishop Herman of Metz (1081)[2]

Gregory, bishop, servant of the servants of God, to [our] beloved brother in Christ, Herman, bishop of Metz: greeting and apostolic benediction.

We do not doubt that what we have learned about your readiness for labors and for dangers that have had to be suffered in defense of truth is of divine gift. It is the ineffable grace and wondrous clemency of this gift that never permits its elect to wander at all, and never allows them to be utterly ruined or cast down; though they may be shaken in time of persecution, the divine gift, by a certain useful testing, toughens them through their fear. Just as among base men fear dispirits the one man when he sees another shamefully flee, so also among strong men one man who acts more bravely than another, who advances more ardently, inflames the manly heart. We have therefore taken care to commend this to Your Charity with the voice of exhortation so that you may delight in standing among the foremost on the battle line of the Christian religion all the more, as you know beyond doubt that they are the nearest and most worthy to God the Victor.

You have asked that you be helped and fortified, as it were, with our letters against the madness of them who gabble with a wicked tongue that the authority of the holy and apostolic See could not excommunicate King Henry, a man, a mocker of Christian law, a destroyer that is of churches and of the Empire, and an

[2] From E. Caspar (ed.), *Das Register Gregors VII* (Berlin, 1920–1923), Reg. VIII, 21: pp. 544–562. Translated by Karl F. Morrison.

author and abetter of heretics; and that it could not absolve anyone from an oath of fidelity to him. This seems to us not entirely necessary, however, since so many very certain testimonies to this fact may be found in the pages of the Holy Scriptures. Nor do we believe that those who impudently detract from and withstand truth, compounding their own damnation, have enforced the brazenness of their defense with these thoughts so much through ignorance as through the hysteria of wretched despair. No wonder; for it is the practice of reprobates, in protecting their wickedness, to undertake defense of men like themselves, since they consider it of no account to incur the destructiveness of falsehood.

For to say a few things about many, who does not know the voice of our Lord and Savior, Jesus Christ, saying in the Gospel, "Thou art Peter, and upon this rock I shall build my Church and the gates of Hell shall not prevail against it, and to you I shall give the keys of the kingdom of heaven; and whatsoever you shall bind on earth shall be bound also in heaven, and whatsoever you shall loose upon earth will be loosed also in heaven." Are kings excepted here, or are they not of the flocks which the Son of God committed to St. Peter? Who, I ask, thinks he has been excluded from the power of Peter in this universal concession of binding and loosing, except perhaps that unhappy man who, unwilling to bear the Lord's yoke, submits himself to the devil's burden and refuses to be in the number of Christ's flock? It profits him very little, for his miserable freedom, to have struck off from his proud neck the power divinely ceded to Saint Peter, since the more anyone through arrogance fights against it, the more heavily he bears it in judgment to his own damnation.

This institution of divine will, therefore, this foundation of the Church's dispensation, this privilege principally given and confirmed to St. Peter, prince of the Apostles, by heavenly decree, the holy Fathers have received with great veneration and kept when they called the holy Roman church, "universal mother," both in general councils, and in other writings and in their deeds. And when they accepted her testimonies in confirmation of the faith and in the understanding of sacred religion, as also her judgments, they agreed on this and assented as though with one spirit and one voice: that all greater matters and important business, and also the judgments of all churches, ought to be referred to her as to a mother and head; that they could never be appealed from her; and that no one ought or could reconsider or refute her judgments.

Wherefore, St. Gelasius, the pope, writing to the Emperor Anastasius, sustained by divine authority, taught him what and how he ought to feel about the principate of the holy and Apostolic See. "Although," he said, "it is right for the necks of the faithful to bend generally before all priests who think rightly about divine matters, how much more must acquiescence be shown to the pontiff of this see, whom Supreme Divinity willed to stand above all priests and, conforming to it, the general piety of the Church has perpetually honored. Wherefore, Your Prudence clearly knows that no one, by any human counsel at all, can ever make himself equal to the privilege and confession of him whom the voice of Christ exalted above all, whom the venerable Church has always confessed and has, in her devotion, as her head." Pope Julius, also, writing to the eastern bishops about the power of this same holy and Apostolic See, says: "It had befitted you, brethren, to speak accurately, and not ironically, in regard to the holy Roman and apostolic church, since even our Lord Jesus Christ having addressed her honorably says: 'Thou art Peter, and upon this rock I shall build my church and the gates of hell shall not prevail against it; and to you I shall give the keys of the kingdom of heaven.' For, by a singular privilege, the power was granted her to open and close the gates of the heavenly kingdom to whomever she wishes." The power of opening and closing heaven has been given her, therefore, and is she not allowed to judge of the earth?

It could not be so. Do you not recall what the most blessed Apostle Paul says: "Do you not know that we shall judge angels? How much more worldly things." St. Gregory the pope also established that kings fell from their office if they presumed to violate decrees of the Apostolic See, writing to a certain Abbot Senator in these words: "But if any king, priest, judge, or secular person knowing this text of our constitution be tempted to go against it, let him lose the dignity of his power and honor, and let him know that, for the iniquity he perpetrated, he stands culpable by divine judgment; and unless he restores whatever he wickedly stole, or, with suitable penance, laments what he has illicitly done, let him be alien to the most holy body and blood of the Lord, our Redeemer, Jesus Christ, and let him fall under severe retribution in the eternal scrutiny."

But if St. Gregory, on all counts a most gentle doctor, decreed that kings who violated his statutes concerning one travelers' inn not only be deposed but also be excommunicated and damned in the eternal scrutiny, who can reprove us for having deposed and excommunicated Henry—a man who not only scorns apostolic judgments, but also tramples his mother the Church under foot in as far as he can, preys most shamelessly on and

destroys most cruelly the whole kingdom and churches—unless perchance it be a man like him? We have learned this from the teaching of St. Peter, in a letter on the ordination of Clement, in which he speaks as follows: "If anyone be a friend to those to whom he"—speaking of the same Clement—"does not speak, he is himself one of them who wish to exterminate the Church of God; and, although he seems to be with us in his body, in mind and soul he is against us, and he is a far more evil foe than those who are outside and clearly enemies. For he does hostile acts under the guise of friendships, and scatters and devastates the Church." Note, therefore, most beloved, that, if he imposes such a grave judgment on a man who, by friendship or discourse, associates with those whom the pope opposes for their acts, with how great a punishment he condemns the very man he opposes for his own acts.

But to come back to the subject: is the office invented even by men ignorant of God not subject to that office which the providence of omnipotent God invented to His honor and mercifully bestowed upon the world? Just as His Son is unhesitatingly believed to be God and man, so also He is considered the High Priest, the head of all priests, sitting at the right hand of the Father and always interceding for us. He despised worldly kingship, on account of which the sons of the world vaunt themselves, and came voluntarily to the priesthood of the Cross. Who does not know that kings and dukes had their beginning from those, ignorant of God, who with blind greed and intolerable presumption strove at the agitation of the prince of the world, namely the devil, to dominate their equals, that is men, through pride, rapines, perfidy, murders, and finally by nearly all sorts of crimes. Indeed, when they constrain priests of the

Lord to bow down to their footsteps, with whom may they more correctly be compared than with him who is the head over all the sons of pride? Tempting the High Priest Himself, the head of priests, the Son of the Most High, and promising Him all the kingdoms of the earth, he says: "All these I shall give to you if you fall down and adore me."

Who doubts that the priests of Christ are counted fathers and masters of kings and princes and all faithful people? Is it not acknowledged to be pitiable madness if a son strives to subjugate his father to himself—or a disciple, his master—and to subject to his power with iniquitous obligations a man by whom he believes he can be bound and loosed not only on earth, but also in Heaven? As St. Gregory recalls in the letter sent to the Emperor Maurice, the Emperor Constantine the Great, lord of all kings and princes and of almost the whole earth, clearly understood these things in the holy Nicene synod: sitting last after all the bishops, he did not presume to give any sentence of judgment on them, but, calling them gods, he judged that they were not under his jurisdiction, but that he hung on their decision. When he was persuading the aforementioned Emperor Anastasius not to consider as an injury the truth that was imparted to his senses, the previously cited Pope Gelasius went on, saying: "There are indeed two, Emperor Augustus, by which this world is principally ruled, the hallowed authority of pontiffs and the royal power. Between them, the weight of the priests is the heavier, inasmuch as they are to render account even for those same kings in the divine scrutiny." And, after interposing a few things, he said, "Know therefore that in these things you hang on their judgment, and that they are unwilling to be governed according to your will."

Supported therefore by such establishments and by such authorities, many pontiffs have excommunicated—some of them kings, others, emperors. For if some special example be required concerning the persons of princes, St. Innocent the pope excommunicated the Emperor Arcadius because he agreed that St. John Chrysostom be expelled from his see. Again, another Roman pontiff deposed a king of the Franks, not indeed because of his iniquities, but because he was not of advantage in such great power, and substituted in his place Pippin, father of the emperor Charlemagne, and absolved all men belonging to the Frankish tribe of the oath of fidelity which they had made to the deposed king. This also holy Church often does by regular authority when it absolves knights of the bond of the oath made to those bishops who have been deposed by apostolic authority from pontifical rank. And St. Ambrose, although a saint, still not universal bishop of the Church, excluded the Emperor Theodosius the Great from the Church, excommunicating him for a wrong which, in the eyes of other bishops, was not so grave. He also in his writings shows that the degree by which gold is more precious than lead is less than that by which the episcopal office is loftier than the royal power. He writes in this fashion toward the beginning of his pastoral book: "The episcopal honor, brethren, and its sublimity can be equated with no comparatives. If you compare it with the splendor of kings and the diadem of princes, they would be as far inferior as if you compared the metallic hue of lead with the splendor of gold; indeed, you may see the necks of kings and princes bowed to the knees of priests, and, having kissed their right hand, they believe that they are strengthened by their prayers."

And, after a few things, "You ought to know, brethren, that we have said all these things first to show that there is nothing in this world more excellent than priests, that nothing is found more sublime than bishops."

Your Fraternity ought to have remembered that the power of an exorcist is conceded to be greater—since he is established a spiritual emperor to cast out demons—than what the cause of worldly dominion can bestow on any layman. Surely demons—alas, more's the pity—lord it over all kings and princes of the earth who do not live religiously and in their acts do not fear God as is meet; and they confound them in wretched servitude. For such men do not wish to have command as religious priests do, led by divine love to the honor of God and the utility of souls; but they strive to dominate others so as to display their pride and fulfill the lust of their soul. Of them, St. Augustine says in his first book on Christian doctrine, "But when someone strives to dominate those who are naturally his equals, that is men, it is indeed unbearable pride." But, furthermore, exorcists, as we have said, have command (*imperium*) from God over demons; how much more, therefore, over them who are subject to demons and the members of demons? If therefore exorcists are so much more exalted than these, how much more yet are priests?

Besides, every Christian king, coming to his end, suppliant and pitiable, requires the work of a priest so that he may evade the prison of Hell, turn from the darkness into the light, and appear in God's judgment absolved of the bonds of sin. But who—not only among priests, but even among laymen—finding himself at the end has implored the help of an earthly king for the salvation of his soul? But

what king or emperor, by virtue of the office imposed upon him, can tear any Christian from the devil's power by holy baptism and number him among the sons of God, and fortify him with holy chrism? And, what is of greatest moment in the Christian religion, who among them can with his own mouth make the body and blood of the Lord, and to which of them has been given the power of binding and loosing in heaven and on earth?

From these proofs it is patently inferred by what great power the office of priests excells Or which of them can ordain any cleric in holy Church? How much less could a king depose him for some wrong? For in ecclesiastical orders, deposition belongs to a higher power than ordaining. Bishops can ordain other bishops, but in no way can they depose them without the authority of the Apostolic See. What smatterer, therefore, can airily doubt that priests take precedence of kings? And if kings are to be judged for their sins by priests, by whom ought they more rightly to be judged than by the Roman pontiff?

To summarize: It is right to understand that any good Christians are kings more appropriately than bad princes. For in seeking God's glory, the former rule themselves rigorously, but, seeking for themselves not what are God's but their own things, the latter tyrannically oppress others as enemies. The first are the body of the true king, Christ; but the others are that of the devil. Good Christians command themselves to this end, that they may rule eternally with the supreme Emperor. But the power of wicked princes does it to the end that they may perish with the prince of darkness, who is king over all the sons of pride.

Indeed, it is far from astonishing that wicked pontiffs concur with an evil king, whom they love and fear because of honors gotten wickedly through him; by ordaining simoniacally anybody who comes along they even sell God at a cheap price. For as the elect are indissolubly united to their head, so also the reprobates are brazenly leagued with him who is the head of malice, especially against the good. To be sure, we should not argue against these men so much as bewail them with tearful laments, so that omnipotent God may snatch them from the snares of Satan, by which they are held captive, and at last lead them, after dangers, to knowledge of truth.

So much for kings and emperors who, thoroughly bloated with worldly glory, rule not for God but for themselves. But since it is our office to allot exortation to each man according to the order or office in which he is seen to live, we take care, motivated by God, to provide the weapons of humility to emperors and kings and other princes so that they may be strong enough to restrain the sea-swells and floods of pride. For we know that earthly glory and worldly care usually draws those most of all who are in commanding positions to swell with pride, inasmuch as having always neglected humility in seeking their own glory, they may wish to stand above the brethren. Therefore, it seems useful [to do this] most of all for emperors and kings so that when their mind finds itself raised on high and is disposed to delight in its singular glory, it may abase itself by these means and it may sense that what gave it happiness is rather to be feared.

Let it therefore diligently perceive how perilous and how fearful is the imperial or royal office in which very few are saved and those who through God's mercy come to salvation are not glorified by the judgment of the Holy Ghost in the Church equally with many paupers. For, from the beginning of the world until these our times, we have not found in the whole of authentic literature seven emperors or kings whose life could be as outstanding in religion and adorned with the virtue of signs as that of the innumerable multitude of them that have despised the world, although we believe that many of them have found the salvation of mercy before omnipotent God. To pass over the Apostles and martyrs, which of the emperors or kings has distinguished himself with miracles to equal Martin, Antony, and Benedict? What emperor or king has raised the dead, purified lepers, or enlightened the blind? Behold, holy Church indeed praises and reveres the Emperor Constantine of pious memory, Theodosius and Honorius, Charles and Louis, lovers of justice, propagators of the Christian religion, and defenders of churches. But it does not declare that they blazed forth with such a great glory of miracles [as the saints]. Moreover, to how many names of kings or emperors has holy Church established that basilicas or altars are to be dedicated, and to the honor of how many of them has it decreed that masses are to be celebrated? Let kings and other princes fear lest, the more they rejoice to have been exalted over men in this life, the more by far they may be laid low beneath the eternal fires. Wherefore, it has been written: "Powerful men powerfully suffer torments." They are to give account to God for as many men as they have subject to their dominion.

But if it is no small labor for one private religious to guard his own soul, how great is the labor incumbent upon princes for many thousands of souls? Further, if the judgment of holy Church strictly binds a sinner for the murder of one man, what will be the case concerning those who give over many thousands to death for the sake of this world's honor? Although they sometimes say *"mea culpa"* with the mouth for killing many men, still they rejoice in the heart for the enlargement of what passes for honor among them; they do not wish that they had not done what they have done; they do not grieve that they have driven their brethren into Tartarus. And since they do not repent with their whole heart and they do not wish to lose what they have gained or held at the cost of human blood, their penitence remains before God without the worthy fruit of penitence. Wherefore, it is indeed to be feared and often recalled to their memory that, as we said before, since the beginning of the world very few kings, in the several kingdoms of the earth, are found to be saints, though the multitude of kings is innumerable. By contrast, in the succession of pontiffs to only one see, namely the Roman, from the time of St. Peter the Apostle, nearly one hundred are counted among the most holy of men. But how could this be, unless the kings of the earth and princes, misled by vainglory, as was said before, prefer their own interests to spiritual matters, while religious pontiffs, on the other hand, despising vainglory, prefer God's interests to fleshly matters. The first readily punish men who offend against them, but in equanimity bear with those who sin against God; the latter quickly forget men who sin against them, but do not lightly pardon those who offend God. The former, thoroughly given over to worldly acts, weigh spiritual concerns lightly; the others, sedulously meditating on heavenly matters, despise those things that are worldly.

All Christians therefore are to be admonished, if they wish to reign with Christ, not to strive to rule with the ambition of worldly power, but rather to have before their eyes what St. Gregory the most holy pope says by way of admonition in his pastoral book: "And so among these things what is to be pursued, what is to be held, except that a man mighty in virtues may be forced to come to government, while one empty of virtues should not be forced to accede." But if men who fear God come under force, with great fear, to the Apostolic See, in which when rightly ordained they are made better men through the merits of St. Peter the Apostle, with how much fear and trembling must one accede to the throne of a kingdom in which even the good and humble, as is known in Saul and David, become worse men? For what we have earlier said about the Apostolic See, although we know it from experience, is thus contained in the decrees of St. Symmachus the pope: "He," that is, St. Peter, "has sent to his successors an everlasting gift of merits with a heritage of innocence." And, after a few things, "For who doubts that he is holy whom the height of so great an office exalts? If good qualities acquired through merit are lacking in him, those suffice which are provided by the earlier tenant of the place. For he either raises brilliant men to these heights or he enlightens those who are raised."

Wherefore, those whom holy Church of her own will calls with deliberate counsel to government or empire, not for transient glory but for the salvation of many, should humbly obey and always beware the witness that St. Gregory bears in the same pastoral book: "Indeed, he becomes like the apostate angel when, though a man, he disdains to be like men. After meritorious humility, Saul thus swelled up in a tumor of pride because of his exalted power. He had been preferred because of humility; because of pride, he was rejected, as the Lord testifies saying:

'When you were but a small child in your eyes, did I not establish you as head among the tribes of Israel?'" And a little further on: "But in an amazing way when he was a small child to himself, he was great to the Lord, but when he seemed great to himself, he was a child to the Lord." And let them vigilantly remember what the Lord says in the Gospel: "I seek not my own glory," and "Whoever wishes to be first among you, let him be the servant of all." Let them always prefer God's honor to their own; let them embrace and guard justice by preserving each man's right for him; let them not go in the counsel of the impious, but with an agreeable heart let them always adhere to the religious. Let them not seek to subdue or subject holy Church to themselves as a handmaiden; but indeed let them fittingly strive to honor her eyes, namely the priests of the Lord, by acknowledging them as masters and fathers. For if we are ordered to honor fleshly fathers and mothers, how much more, spiritual? And if he who curses his fleshly father and mother is to be punished with death, what does the man deserve who curses his spiritual father and mother? Let them not strive, misled by carnal love, to set their son over the flock for which Christ poured out His blood, if they can find one better and more useful to that flock; let them not inflict the greatest damage on holy Church by loving their son more than God. For patently a man is clearly shown not to love God and his neighbor as suits a Christian if he fails to provide as well as he can for the great utility and need of his holy mother, the Church. When this virtue, namely charity, is neglected, whatever good anyone does will lack every fruit of salvation. And so, in humbly doing these things and keeping the love of God and neighbor, as in right, let them

trust in the mercy of Him who said, "Learn of me, for I am meek and lowly of heart." If they humbly imitate Him, they will pass from a servile and transitory realm to one that is truly free and eternal.

Encyclical Letter of Gregory VII (1084) [3]

Gregory, bishop, servant of the servants of God, to all the faithful in Christ who truly love the Apostolic-See: greeting and apostolic benediction.

It has come, dearest brethren, it has come, we think, to your notice that in our day that condition has been renewed which is described by searching in the Psalms: "Why have the nations raged, and the people imagined vain things? The kings of the earth have risen, and the princes have come together as one against the Lord and against His anointed [christum]." For the princes of the nations and the princes of priests have come together as one with a great multitude against Christ, the Son of omnipotent God, and against His Apostle Peter, to extinguish the Christian religion and propagate heretical depravity. But, by God's mercy, they have not been able to deflect those who trust in the Lord to their impiety by any terror, or any cruelty, or the promise of earthly glory. Indeed, the conspirators have iniquitously raised their hands against us for no reason other than that we were unwilling to pass over in silence the danger to holy Church and to them . . . [hiatus in the text], who do not blush to reduce the same spouse of God to servitude. For in all lands even impoverished women of little position are allowed to take a husband legitimately, according to the law of their homeland and according to their own will. But, through the wish

---

[3] From P. Jaffé, *Monumenta Gregoriana* (Berlin, 1865), no. 46: pp. 572–575. Translated by Karl F. Morrison.

and detestable custom of the impious, holy Church, which is the spouse of God and our mother, is not allowed to cleave to her Spouse legally on earth, according to divine law and according to her own will.

For we ought not to suffer the sons of holy Church to be subjected to heretics, adulterers, and intruders as though to fathers, and to be branded by them as with the scandal of adultery. Hence many evils, diverse perils, and unheard-of crimes of cruelty of every sort have arisen, as you can learn more clearly than day and by true account from our legates. And if you truly grieve and are afflicted by the ruin and confusion of the Christian religion, and, touched inwardly by sure anguish, wish to give it a helping hand, you can be sufficiently instructed by them. For they are most faithful to St. Peter and, of his house, they are counted, each in his own order, among the chief men. It has been impossible to withdraw them from his fidelity and defense, or to separate them from the bosom of holy mother Church, by any terror or any promise of temporal things.

But since, as Your Fraternity knows, it was divinely said through the Prophet, though to an unworthy man and a sinner, "Upon a high mountain" and the rest ["Upon a lofty and high mountain hast thou set thy bed; even thither wentest thou up to offer sacrifice."] and again, "Cry out; do not cease," whether I wish to or not, I evangelize, having set aside all modesty, shyness also, and earthly love of anyone. I cry out, cry out, and again cry out, and I declare to you that the Christian religion and the true faith which the Son of God, coming from Heaven, has taught us through our Fathers has been turned into a depraved custom of the world—alas, for grief—it has declined almost to nothing, and, having changed its ancient color, it has fallen to the derision, not only of the devil, but also of the Jews, Saracens, and pagans. For these men keep their laws, as a matter of religious belief, although in this day, their laws do not serve the salvation of souls and have not been illuminated and confirmed by any miracles as our law has been by the frequent witness of the eternal King.

But we, drunk with love of the world and deceived by vain ambition, having neglected all religion and integrity in favor of cupidity and pride, look like outlaws and fools; for we neither have the salvation and honor of present and future life, as our fathers did, nor do we even hope for it, as we should. And while there are some, although they are very rare, who fear God, they struggle with ready will for themselves and not, however, for the common salvation of the brethren. But who, and how many, are they who toil and labor even to the point of death for fear and love of omnipotent God, in whom we live, move, and have our being, as much as worldly soldiers do for their lords, or even for friends and subjects?

Behold, every day, many thousands of secular men run to death for their lords; but for God in heaven, and our Redeemer, they not only fail to run, but they even disdain to endure the enmities of a few men. And if there are some—or rather, by God's mercy there are, but very few indeed—who, for love of Christian law, struggle to resist the impious head-on even to the point of death, they are not helped by the brethren, as is right, and, even more, the imprudent and undiscerning think them mad. But since these matters and others like them touch us especially, as we indicate to you, we ask and beseech in the Lord Jesus, who redeems us by His death, that you strive to know by diligent inquiry the tribulations and distress which we are suffering from the enemies of the Christian religion, and how and in what manner we are suffering, so that we may, by God's dispensation, uproot vices from the hearts of the brethren and plant virtues in them.

For, from the time when the divine mother Church placed me on the apostolic throne, though I was unworthy and, as God is witness, unwilling, I have taken care most of all that holy Church, God's spouse, our lady and mother, returning to her proper repute, should remain free, chaste, and catholic. But since these things entirely displeased the ancient enemy, he armed his members against us to turn everything at odds. Thus he did against us, or rather, against the Apostolic See, such great things as he has been unable to do since the time of Constantine the Great. And no wonder, for the nearer the time of Antichrist approaches, the more he struggles to extinguish the Christian religion.

But now, my dearest brethren, listen diligently to what I am saying to you. Everyone in the whole world who is known by the name of Christian and truly understands the Christian faith knows and believes that St. Peter, the prince of the Apostles, is the father of all Christians and the first pastor after Christ, and that the holy Roman church is the mother and mistress of all churches. If therefore you believe this and hold to it without doubt, I ask you and I command—I, your brother of whatever sort, and unworthy master—by omnipotent God, that you aid and succor your aforesaid father and mother, if you desire to have absolution of all sins from them and blessing and grace in this age and in the one to come. May omnipotent God, from whom all good things proceed, always illumine your mind and enrich it with love of Him and of your neighbor that you may be worthy to make your aforesaid father and mother

your debtors, with sure devotion, and to enter their companionship without shame. Amen.

HENRY IV'S POSITION

Henry's Letter Condemning Gregory VII (1076)[4]

Henry, King not by usurpation, but by the pious ordination of God, to Hildebrand, now not Pope, but false monk:

You have deserved such a salutation as this because of the confusion you have wrought; for you left untouched no order of the Church which you could make a sharer of confusion instead of honor, of malediction instead of benediction.

For to discuss a few outstanding points among many: Not only have you dared to touch the rectors of the holy Church—the archbishops, the bishops, and the priests, anointed of the Lord as they are—but you have trodden them under foot like slaves who know not what their lord may do. In crushing them you have gained for yourself acclaim from the mouth of the rabble. You have judged that all these know nothing, while you alone know everything. In any case, you have sedulously used this knowledge not for edification, but for destruction, so greatly that we may believe Saint Gregory, whose name you have arrogated to yourself, rightly made this prophecy of you when he said: "From the abundance of his subjects, the mind of the prelate is often exalted, and he thinks that he has more knowledge than anyone else, since he sees that he has more power than anyone else."

And we, indeed, bore with all these abuses, since we were eager to preserve the honor of the Apostolic See. But you

---

[4] From T. E. Mommsen and Karl F. Morrison, *Imperial Lives and Letters of the Eleventh Century* (New York: Columbia University Press, 1962), pp. 150–151. Footnotes omitted.

construed our humility as fear, and so you were emboldened to rise up even against the royal power itself, granted to us by God. You dared to threaten to take the kingship away from us—as though we had received the kingship from you, as though kingship and empire were in your hand and not in the hand of God.

Our Lord, Jesus Christ, has called us to kingship, but has not called you to the priesthood. For you have risen by these steps: namely, by cunning, which the monastic profession abhors, to money; by money to favor; by favor to the sword. By the sword you have come to the throne of peace, and from the throne of peace you have destroyed the peace. You have armed subjects against their prelates; you who have not been called by God have taught that our bishops who have been called by God are to be spurned; you have usurped for laymen the bishops' ministry over priests, with the result that these laymen depose and condemn the very men whom the laymen themselves received as teachers from the hand of God, through the imposition of the hands of bishops.

You have also touched me, one who, though unworthy, has been anointed to kingship among the anointed. This wrong you have done to me, although as the tradition of the holy Fathers has taught, I am to be judged by God alone and am not to be deposed for any crime unless—may it never happen—I should deviate from the Faith. For the prudence of the holy bishops entrusted the judgment and the deposition even of Julian the Apostate not to themselves, but to God alone. The true pope Saint Peter also exclaims, "Fear God, honor the king." You, however, since you do not fear God, dishonor me, ordained of Him.

Wherefore, when Saint Paul gave no quarter to an angel from heaven if the angel should preach heterodoxy, he did not except you who are now teaching heterodoxy throughout the earth. For he says, "If anyone, either I or an angel from heaven, preach any other gospel unto you than that which we have preached unto you, let him be accursed." Descend, therefore, condemned by this anathema and by the common judgment of all our bishops and of ourself. Relinquish the Apostolic See which you have arrogated. Let another mount the throne of Saint Peter, another who will not cloak violence with religion but who will teach the pure doctrine of Saint Peter.

I, Henry, King by the grace of God, together with all our bishops, say to you: Descend! Descend!

Decree of the Synod of Brixen (1080)[5]

In the year of the incarnation of the Lord 1080, with the most serene King Henry IV as moderator, in the twenty-sixth year of his reign, on the seventh day before the Kalends of July, on the fifth day of the week, in the third indiction, when an assembly of thirty bishops and of the leaders of the army, not only of Italy but also of Germany, was gathered at Brixen in Bavaria by royal order, of one accord a voice came forth as though from the mouth of all complaining terribly against the cruel madness of one false monk, Hildebrand, also called Pope Gregory VII. It complained that the ever-unconquered King suffered this madness to rage untouched for so long, when Paul, the vessel of election, witnesses that the prince does not carry a sword without cause and Peter, the first of the Apostles, cries out that the king not only is supreme but that governors are to be sent by him

───────────
[5] From T. E. Mommsen and Karl F. Morrison, *Imperial Lives and Letters of the Eleventh Century* (New York: Columbia University Press, 1962), pp. 157–160. Footnotes omitted.

specifically for the punishment of evil-
doers and for the praise of the good. In
fulfillment of these sayings it seemed
just to this most glorious King and to his
princes that the judgment of the bishops
with the sentence of divine censure ought
to issue against this Hildebrand before
the material sword went forth against
him, with the consequence that the royal
power might resolve to prosecute him
with greater freedom after the prelates of
the Church had first deposed him from
his proud prelacy.

Which of the Faithful knowing him
would fear to let fly the shaft of damnation
against him? From the time he entered
the world, this man strove to procure
position for himself over men through
vain glory, without the support of any
merits; to set dreams and divinations, his
own and those of others, ahead of divine
dispensation; to appear a monk in habit
and not to be one by profession; to judge
himself exempt from ecclesiastical discipline, subject to no master; to devote himself more than laymen to obscene theatri-
cal shows; publicly for the sake of filthy
lucre, to attend to the tables of the money
changers on the porch of those who do
business? And so from these pursuits, he
garnered his money and, supplanting the
abbot, usurped the abbacy of Saint Paul.

Thereafter, seizing the archdiaconate,
he led a certain man named Mancius
astray by guile so that man sold him his
own office. And against the will of Pope
Nicholas, a popular tumult attending his
action, he forced his advancement to the
stewardship of Saint Peter's. Finally, he
is convicted of having murdered four
Roman pontiffs with violent deaths. His
instrument was poison administered at
the hands on one of his intimates, namely,
John Braciutus. Although he repented too
late, while others still kept silent this
ministrant of death himself bore witness

to these deeds with dire cries, pressed by
the nearness of his own death. And then,
on the same night in which the funeral
rites of Pope Alexander were lovingly
performed in the basilica of the Savior,
this oft-mentioned plague-bearer fortified
the gates of the Roman city and the brid-
ges, the towers and the triumphal arches,
with detachments of armed men. When a
military force had been brought together,
like an enemy he occupied the Lateran
Palace. And lest the clergy should dare
oppose him, since no one wished to elect
him, he terrified them by threatening
them with death upon the unsheathed
swords of his followers. He sprang upon
the long-occupied throne before the body
of the dead man reached its tomb. But
when certain of the clergy wanted to remind him of the decree of Pope Nicholas
(which was promulgated with the threat
of anathema by one hundred twenty-five
bishops and with the approval of this same
Hildebrand and which stated that if anyone presumed to be pope without the assent of the Roman prince, he should be
considered by all not pope, but an apostate), he denied that he knew there was a
king anywhere, and he asserted that he
could adjudge the decrees of his predecessors void.

What more? Not only Rome, indeed,
but the Roman world itself, bears witness
that he has not been elected by God but
that he has most impudently thrust himself upward through force, fraud, and
money. His fruits reveal his root; his
words show his intent. He it was who subverted ecclesiastical order, who threw the
rule of the Christian empire into turmoil,
who plotted death of body and soul for the
catholic and pacific King, who defended
a king who was a breaker of vows and a
traitor, who sowed discord among those
in concord, strife among the peaceful,
scandals among brothers, divorce among

the married, and who shook whatever was seen to stand in quiet amidst those who lived piously.

Wherefore, as was said before, we who have been gathered together through the agency of God, supported by the legates and letters of the nineteen bishops who assembled at Mainz on the holy day of last Pentecost, pass judgment against that same most insolent Hildebrand: for he preaches acts of sacrilege and arson; he defends perjuries and murders; long a disciple of the heretic Beringer, he places in question the catholic and apostolic Faith in regard to the Body and Blood of the Lord; he is an open devotée of divinations and dreams, and a necromancer working with an oracular spirit; and therefore he wanders beyond the limits of the true Faith. We judge that canonically he must be deposed and expelled and that, unless he descends from this See after hearing these words, he is forever damned.

I, Hugh Candidus, cardinal priest of the holy Roman Church, from the Title of Saint Clement in the third district of the city, have assented to this decree promulgated by us, and I have subscribed it in the name of all the Roman cardinals.

I, Diepold, archbishop of Milan, have subscribed.

I, Kuono, bishop of Brescia, have subscribed.

I, Otto, bishop-elect of Tortona, have subscribed.

I, William, bishop of Pavia, have subscribed.

I, Reginald, bishop of Belluno, have subscribed.

I, Sigebod, bishop of Verona, have subscribed.

I, Dionysius, bishop of Piacenza, have subscribed.

Udo, bishop of Asti. I have subscribed.

I, Hugh, bishop-elect of Firmo, have subscribed.

Milo of Padua has subscribed.

I, Conrad, bishop of Utrecht, have subscribed.

Henry, the patriarch [of Aquileia], has subscribed.

Didald, bishop of Vicenza, has subscribed.

Regenger, bishop of Vercelli, has subscribed.

Rupert, bishop of Bamberg, has subscribed.

Norbert, bishop of Chur, has subscribed.

Eberhard, bishop of Parma, has subscribed.

Roland, by the grace of God, bishop of Treviso, most willingly has subscribed.

Arnold, bishop of Cremona, has subscribed.

Arnold, bishop of Bergamo, has subscribed.

I, Diedo, bishop of Brandenburg, have subscribed.

Leomar, archbishop of the holy church of Hamburg.

I, Werner, by the grace of God, bishop of Bobbio, have subscribed.

I, Altwin, bishop of Brixen, have subscribed.

I, Meginward, bishop of Freising, have subscribed.

I, Burchard, bishop of Lausanne, have subscribed.

I, Conrad, bishop of Genoa, have subscribed.

Henry, King by the grace of God. I have subscribed.

GERHART B. LADNER (b. 1905) has earned distinction both as a student of art and as an expositor of the history of ideas. He began his career at the University of Vienna (Ph.D., 1930), and he was able to continue his studies in Vienna and in Rome until 1938. The two principal works of these years—*Theologie und Politik vor dem Investiturstreit* (1936) and *I ritratti dei papi nell'Antichità e nel Medioevo*. vol. I (1941)— proved his virtuosity in art history and in the history of ideas. The earlier of these books also established Ladner's abiding interest in the Investiture Controversy, which is to achieve its most ample exposition in the second volume of his brilliant work *The Idea of Reform* (vol. I, 1959). The following essay provides a masterful preliminary analysis of Gregory VII's dominant views.*

Gerhart B. Ladner

Gregory Sought to Revive the Ancient Spirit of the Church

In the study of the Gregorian Church Reform, little attention has been paid to the origin and meaning of the term and idea of reform and to related concepts, as understood by the reformers themselves. Yet here, as elsewhere, awareness of the self-interpretation of a historical movement is a prerequisite (though not a guarantee) for our own understanding of it. If some modern interpreters of the Gregorian age would characterize it as a period of revolution rather than of reform, such uncertainties of terminology are no doubt due to insufficient investigation of the Gregorian renewal concepts and of the tradition out of which they grew.

Actually, the term *reformare* [reform] occurs less frequently in Gregory VII's letters than other renewal terms, such as *renovare, restaurare* [renew, restore], etc., which, however, do not essentially differ from the meaning of the concept of reform. The idea of renewal in the sense of revolution, that is to say, of untraditional innovation, is explicitly rejected by the Pope.

An analysis of two rarely quoted documents of the Gregorian era—at least one of them by Gregory VII himself—seems to open a new approach to the whole field of Gregorian renewal ideas.

I

In his *Historia Mediolanensis* [History of Milan], Landulf of St. Paul has preserved a letter which Gregory VII in 1075

*Gerhart B. Ladner, "Two Gregorian Letters on the Sources and Nature of Gregory VII's Reform Ideology," *Studi Gregoriani,* 5 (1956), 221–242. Reprinted by permission of the author and of Abbazia di San Paolo di Roma, Via Ostiense 186, Rome. Footnotes omitted.

had written to Landulf's uncle, the priest Liutprand, a leader of the Milanese Pataria movement. During the Patarene uprising against the feudalized Church dignitaries of Milan, Liutprand (Liprandus) had been brutally mutilated. His ears and nose had been cut off. The Pope wrote him a letter of consolation and commendation, which Liutprand preserved as a sort of talisman in his later struggles with Archbishop Grosulanus of Milan. Gregory in this letter reminds the priest of the sufferings of the saints, of their passions and mutilations. He compares Liutprand with the martyrs of the past, and says that, in spite of the "diminution" of his body, his "inward man is renewed day by day" (2 Cor. 4, 16) and has greatly increased in holiness. Liutprand may look ugly, but the image of God in him has become more beautiful.

Si sanctorum memoriam veneramur de quorum legimus morte et abscissione membrorum . . . , tu quoque absciso naso et auribus pro Christi nomine laudabilior es . . . Integritas quidem corporis tui diminuta est, sed interior homo qui renovatur de die in diem (2 Cor. 4, 16), magnum sanctitatis suscepit incrementum; forma visibilis turpior, sed imago Dei, quae est forma iustitiae, facta est in diminutione iocundior, in turpitudine pulchrior . . .[1]

This text is of considerable interest because it clearly reveals the Pauline roots of Gregory VII's renewal terminology and

ideology. This dependence goes far beyond the direct quotation of 2 Cor. 4, 16. The reference to the *imago Dei* [image of God] links Gregory's thought to several other Pauline texts in which man's renewal through Christ is conceived of as the renovation or reformation of his original image-likeness with God, according to Gen. 1, 26. Gregory VII is here not only a disciple of the Apostle, but also stands in a long and uninterrupted tradition which extends from the Fathers to his own times and beyond. It is noteworthy that the Pope sees the Milanese priest's efforts and sufferings for the cause of Church reform in terms of the renewal of the image of God in man. This constitutes a tie to the old and never lost tradition of Christian renewal as that of individual persons. On the other hand, from Gregory VII onward, papal letters frequently express the idea of a reform of the laws of the Church, of specific churches, and of the Church as a whole. It was only in the Gregorian period that the universal Church became fully conscious, as it were, in the minds of its reformers of the possibility and necessity of its perpetual self-reform, fully conscious also of the fact that the reform of the Church as an institution was part and parcel of papal primacy. A little known fragment from a letter ascribed to Gregory VII, and in any case belonging to the Gregorian age, shows how this realization is related to another aspect of early Christian renewal ideology.

II

Ivo of Chartres in his *Decretum* IV, 213, has the following text:

Usum qui veritati contrarius est abolendum esse.

Gregorius VII Wimundo Aversano episcopo.

Si consuetudinem fortassis opponas, advertendum fuerit quod Dominus dicit: Ego sum veritas et vita (cf. John 14, 6). Non ait: Ego sum

---

[1] [If we revere the memory of the saints about whose deaths and dismemberment we read . . . , you also are the more worthy of praise since your nose and ears have been cut off for the name of Christ. . . . The wholeness of your body, indeed, has been diminished, but the man within, who is renewed from day to day (2 Cor. 4:16), has received a great increase of holiness: the visible form is more unsightly, but the image of God, which is the form of justice, has become the more pleasing in diminution, the more comely in unsightliness . . .—Ed.]

P. Jaffé ed., *Bibliotheca Rerum Germanicarum*, vol. 2: *Monumenta Gregoriana* (Berlin, 1865), p. 533 f., nr. 12.

consuetudo, sed veritas. Et certe, ut beati
Cypriani utamur sententia, quaelibet consuetudo, quantumvis vetusta, quantumvis vul-
gata, veritati est omnino postponenda et usus
qui veritati est contrarius abolendus[2]

Here, one of Christ's greatest words, "I
am the way, and the truth, and the life"
(John 14, 6), is contrasted in unforgettable
terseness with something which He definitely never said: I am custom. From the
positing of this contrast there follows the
conclusion (supported also by a reference
to St. Cyprian) that even the oldest and
most wide-spread custom must be abolished, if it is contrary to the truth.

The same fragment with only very minor variations and with the same inscription "Gregory VII to Bishop Guitmund of
Aversa," occurs in the other Ivonian collections, that is to say, in the *Panormia*
and in the third part of the *Collectio
Trium Partium* and is found also in Gratian's *Decretum* D. VIII, c. 5. The text
(henceforth quoted by its JL number 5277)[3]
raises three problems. First: is it rightly
attributed to Gregory VII? Second: what
is its relation to St. Cyprian, to the Council of Carthage of September 1, 256, and to
St. Augustine, respectively? Third: how
does it illustrate Gregorian reform ideology?

P. Kehr is most probably right, in point-
ing out that the inscription of JL 5277
must be somehow vitiated; for, there is

little doubt that Guitmund was made
Bishop of Aversa only by Urban II. Nevertheless, there remains the distinct possibility that the letter was in fact addressed
by Gregory VII to Guitmund before he
became bishop and that Ivo not unnatu-
rally gave him the rank which he had
since attained. One hesitates to assume
without cogent reason that an almost contemporary source is in error; besides,
Guitmund's relations with the Gregorian
Church reform in its earlier stages and
with Gregory VII himself are well docu-
mented. He was a monk of La Croix-
Saint Leufroi, a Norman monastery then
closely connected with St. Ouen at Rouen,
which itself played a certain role in the
spreading of Cluniac influence to Normandy brought about by the great reformer St. William of Dijon. Guitmund
then became a disciple of Lanfranc at
Bec, another Cluniac reform focus in
Normandy, and between 1073 and 1078
followed his master's example in writing
a famous treatise against Berengar of
Tours' eucharistic heresy, which may
well have drawn him to Gregory's attention. If Ordericus Vitalis is correct,
William the Conqueror called Guitmund
to England and wanted to confer a
bishopric upon him; but he did not
accept, and he seems to have rebuked the
king in good Augustinian-Gregorian fashion by telling him that his conquest of
England, taken in itself, was nothing but
a great brigandage *(rapina, praeda)*, and
that William would continue to rule only
as long as it was pleasing to God. Perhaps,
about that time he began to call himself
simply "a Christian," *Christianus*, rather
than *Guitmundus*, thus expressing a re-
vitalized concept of Christianitas, characteristic for Gregory VII and his age. By
1077, Guitmund had left Normandy and
probably gone to Rome, as in that year he
was sent together with two of Gregory
VII's legates, Cardinal Bernard and Ab-

---

[2][*The usage that is contrary
to truth must be abolished.*

Gregory VII to Bishop Guitmund of Aversa.

If perchance you adduce custom, you should pay
attention to what the Lord says: "I am truth and life"
(cf. John 14:6). He does not say, "I am custom," but
"truth." And surely, to use the judgment of St. Cyprian, any custom—however old, however common
—must be utterly subordinated to truth, and a usage
that is contrary to truth must be abolished.—Ed.]

Ivo of Chartres, *Decretum*, IV, 213, J. P. Migne,
Patrologiae Cursus Completus, series Latina, vol.
161, col. 311.

[3]JL is an abbreviation for Jaffé-Loewenfeld, *Regesta Pontificum Romanorum*.

bot Bernard of St. Victor at Marseille to the Synod of Forchheim (March 1077), which was meant to decide whether Henry IV or Rudolf of Swabia should be King of Germany. On their way back from Germany, Bernard of St. Victor and Christianus, i.e. Guitmund, were captured by a follower of Henry IV, Count Ulrich of Lenzburg. After their liberation, they remained almost a year in the Black Forest monastery of Hirsau, and it is well known that the adaptation of the monastic consuetudines of Hirsau to those of Cluny dates from that visit of the Cluniac Bernard of Marseille (followed by a visit of Udalric of Cluny) and that from that time onward Hirsau became the most important Gregorian reform center in Germany; the sources say nothing about a share of Guitmund in the reform of Hirsau, but having been subject to Cluniac influence he, too, may have contributed to this crucial propagation of the Cluniac-Gregorian spirit in Germany. It is uncertain when exactly Guitmund returned to Rome; it is not improbable that he had a part in the Roman proceedings of 1078–79, which led to the final condemnation of Berengar by Gregory VII at the Lenten Synod held at Rome in 1079. In 1083, Guitmund took part on the papal side in the unsuccessful three-cornered peace negotiations between the Romans and the representatives of Henry IV and Gregory VII. After Gregory VII's death, Guitmund seems to have manifested his strictly Gregorian point of view by opposing Pope Victor III (Desiderius of Monte Cassino), who had compromised with Henry IV.

It would, then, be by no means surprising if Gregory VII had written Guitmund a letter containing a strong statement of principle such as that preserved in JL 5277. One might, for instance, surmise that this letter was addressed to Guitmund on the occasion of the legation to Forchheim when in connection with Gregorian argumentation against Henry IV the stressing of truth as superior to custom would have been very appropriate and in accordance with the Pope's other utterances on the king's case (see below pp. 57f, 59). That the nonobligatory character of uncanonical customs and the impossibility of compromising with them were stressed in the Gregorian camp, can be seen also from Bernold of St. Blasien's *Apologeticus* for Gregory's Roman reform council of 1074, where Bernold explains that the Pope could not condone *consuetudines* [customs] if to do so meant to ignore sanctions on behalf of which the saints had suffered.

Fortassis autem aliquis dicit cur noster Gregorius tam contraria nostrae consuetudini statuta observari praeceperit, cur non potius nostram consuetudinem quasi misericordi dissimulatione tolerarit . . . Dicat ergo quivis quomodo noster apostolicus . . . negligere possit quin . . . sanctionum . . . impugnatoribus . . . obviaret, quibus ipsos sanctos patres usque ad sanguinem restitisse non ignoraret.[4]

It is, of course, not impossible that Ivo did make a mistake and that JL 5277 was addressed to Guitmund as Bishop of Aversa by Urban II (a later Pope is excluded if Guitmund was the addressee—and there is no reason to doubt it—since Bernold of St. Blasien writing in 1088 speaks of Christianus, i.e. of Guitmund, as Bishop, and since John, his successor in the see of Aversa, appears during Urban's pontificate). Whether the author of JL 5277 was Gregory or Urban, its gen-

---

[4] [But perhaps someone is saying, "Why should our Gregory command that statutes so opposed to our custom be observed? Why should he not, rather, bear with our custom with dissimulation, as if in mercy?" . . . Let therefore such a person say how our *Apostolicus* . . . could fail to withstand men assailing the sanctions . . . for which, he knows, the holy Fathers stood up to the death.—Ed.]

Apologeticus, 20. *Monumenta Germaniae Historica, Libelli de lite*, vol. 2, p. 84.

uineness and its date in the age of the Gregorian Church reform are vouched for by an almost identical passage in Urban II's letter to Robert I of Flanders of 1092. There the Pope tells the Count that the old usage or custom of his country (Urban refers especially to Robert, but no doubt has in mind also the feudal lords in general), according to which the estate of deceased clerics is appropriated by seculars, cannot stand:

Quod si praetendis hoc ex antiquo usu in terra tua processisse, scire debes creatorem tuum dixisse: Ego sum veritas, non autem usus vel consuetudo.[5]

JL 5277, as noted above, is chapter 213 in the fourth part of Ivo's *Decretum,* which in its first sixty chapters deals with feasts and fasting and then with the canonical scriptures, approved works of ecclesiastical writers, laws, tradition and custom *(consuetudines),* and with the celebration of councils. Among the chapters on custom, there also are several extracts from St. Augustine among which *Decretum* IV, 208, 209, 234, and 235, taken from Augustine's *De baptismo contra Donatistas,* are particularly important in our context. Ivo's chapter 234 is the one most closely related to Ivo's chapter 213, i.e., to JL 5277. The second sentence of c. 234 is an almost literal quotation from Augustine's *De baptismo* III, 6 (9), where Augustine himself quotes Bishop Libosus of Vaga who was present at the Cyprianian Council of Carthage of September 1, 256 (see below). This Ivonian quotation from Augustine reads as follows:

Nam Dominus in evangelio: Ego sum, inquit, veritas. Non dixit: Ego sum consuetudo.[6]

It is almost identical with the second half of the first sentence of JL 5277, attributed by Ivo to Gregory VII; JL 5277, however, according to the Ivonian fragment, does not mention Augustine, but in the following sentence refers to Cyprian. This is easily explained by the fact that Augustine in *De baptismo* continually cites Cyprian, though in the particular text in question, as just mentioned, he quotes Libosus of Vaga, i.e. the *Sententiae episcoporum numero LXXXVII de haereticis baptizandis* of the Carthaginian Council of September, 256, which was held under Cyprian's presidency. *Sententia* 30, pronounced by the Bishop of Vaga, states:

In evangelio Dominus: Ego sum, inquit, veritas. Non dixit: Ego sum consuetudo. Itaque veritate manifestata cedat consuetudo veritati, ut etsi in praeteritum quis in ecclesia haereticos non baptizabat, nunc baptizare incipiat.[7]

Cyprian himself, in his letter to Pomponius, dealing with the same matter of the baptism of heretics, had used John 14, 6 in the same manner:

Nam consuetudo sine veritate vetustas erroris est . . . Quam veritatem nobis Christus ostendens in evangelio dicit: Ego sum veritas.[8]

But it was not even Cyprian who had invented the striking formula. This honour seems to go to the *homo terribilis* of west-

---

[5] [But if you pretend that this derives from ancient usage in your land, you ought to know that your Creator has said: "I am truth," but not "usage" or "custom."—Ed.]
Jaffé-Loewenfeld, *Regesta Pontificum Romanorum,* nr. 5471.

[6] [For the Lord said in the Gospel: "I am truth." He did not say: "I am custom."—Ed.]

[7] [In the Gospel, the Lord said, "I am truth." He did not say, "I am custom." Therefore, since truth had been made manifest, custom gave way to truth, so that, although in the past one did not baptize heretics in Church, now one began to baptize them.—Ed.]
Cyprian, *Opera Omnia, Corpus Scriptorum Ecclesiasticorum Latinorum,* vol. 3, part 1, p. 448.

[8] [For custom without truth is antiquity of error . . . showing which truth to us, Christ says in the Gospel, "I am truth."—Ed.]
Ibid., p. 806f. (ep. LXXIV, 9).

ern patristics who had contributed so much also otherwise to the Latin expression of early Christian doctrine: to Tertullian. In his *De virginibus velandis,* he writes that virgins ought to be veiled. This, he says, is "the truth of the matter," though contrary custom, initiated by ignorance or simpleness of mind and perpetuated by continuous use may be alleged against it. And he closes:

Sed Dominus noster Christus veritatem se non consuetudinem cognominavit.[9]

The old African dictum, since it is utilized in JL 5277 and also in Urban's letter of 1092 to Robert of Flanders, must have been known to the papal chancery of the Gregorian reform period; in other words, Ivo could find it not only in St. Cyprian and St. Augustine or in patristic florilegia, but also in documents of contemporary or near-contemporary Popes. Whether the papal chancery under Gregory VII or Urban II had itself gone as far back as Cyprian (Tertullian's works were certainly not used directly at the time) or had relied on St. Augustine's *De baptismo* and on florilegia, is impossible to decide. The phrase in JL 5277: *ut beati Cypriani utamur sententia* [to use the sentence of St. Cyprian], was, perhaps, not meant to be taken literally, since it seems that only the content but not the exact wording of the remainder of JL 5277 is Cyprianian. Yet, direct use of Cyprian by Gregory VII or Urban II need not be excluded, in spite of the conflict between Africa and Rome over the baptism of heretics in Cyprian's time; the anti-Roman sting of that controversy had been taken out by Augustine, especially through that very book *De baptismo,* quoted by Ivo, which in many of its chapters constitutes a thorough re-in-

terpretation of Cyprian, and the writings of the venerated martyr bishop, who is one of the few non-Roman saints mentioned in the Canon of the Mass, were in wide circulation since Christian Antiquity.

The Tertullianean-Cyprianian-Augustinian principle, resuscitated by JL 5277, that truth is superior to custom, was of the greatest actuality for the Gregorian reform movement; but, so was the rejection of untraditional innovation, enunciated against Cyprian in the baptismal controversy by Pope Stephen I: *nihil innovetur nisi quod traditum est* [let nothing be introduced except what has been handed down]. These two principles are like the obverse and the reverse of a single coin. As already Cyprian had asserted and Augustine had formulated more clearly, they are not essentially opposed to one another. The question is rather whether or not a custom is in conformity with the truth and its truthful tradition. If it is not, it must be re-formed. This reform is not an innovation which would violate tradition, in the sense of Stephen I's objections to Cyprian on the particular question then debated, but it is the undoing of such innovations in favor of customs which are in accordance with truth and tradition. To build a bridge from the old truth to acceptable customs of the present across half a millennium of inveterate "bad customs," was in fact the problem and aim of the Gregorian reform.

III

Notwithstanding his assertion that the Pope may issue new laws whenever necessary, Gregory VII never tired to repeat that he was not an untraditional "innovator," that he had not come to set up new customs in the Church, only to renew the old and true ones. This intention may be considered to form the supra-individual

---

[9] [But our Lord Christ called himself truth, not custom.—Ed.]

Migne, *PL,* vol. 2, col. 936f

meaning of his reform concept beside the individual one discussed in the first section of this paper.

All through Gregory VII's pontificate, his letters furnish evidence of the role which the antithetical concepts of *canonical truth* (termed *veritas,* but also *doctrina sanctorum patrum, divina lex* [doctrine of the holy Fathers, divine law], etc.) and of *evil custom* (*consuetudo,* which may be "old," and yet an unjustifiable "invention," an offense against the still older truth) played in the Pope's thought. To mention a few examples: in a letter concerning the consecration of the Bishop of Dol by the Pope himself, he holds the *statuta sanctorum patrum* [statutes of the holy Fathers] against the inveterate and most evil custom *(antiqua et pessima consuetudo)* of lay investiture and simony; similarly, he objects to Henry IV's, defense of *consuetudines* invented against the liberty of the Church, the king should rather observe *sanctorum patrum doctrinam* [doctrine of the holy Fathers], i.e. ancient canon law; and in a pathetic appeal to all the faithful written shortly before the end, he complains that the *vera fides* [true faith] has been replaced by the depraved custom of the world *(secularis prava consuetudo).*

Such antitheses are paralleled in Gregory's correspondence by the contrast between the concepts of unjust or untraditional and, therefore, evil *new custom* (*nova consuetudo, contra catholicam fidem inserta* [new custom, intruded contrary to catholic faith], etc.) and of canonical *old custom* (*prisca consuetudo, antiquus mos, vetus auctoritas sanctorum patrum* [pristine custom, ancient practice, early authority of the holy Fathers], etc.). So, for instance, he reproaches the Bishop of Verdun for trying to force new customs *(novas consuetudines)* upon the monastery of St. Mihiel, even though he has been admonished to make only canonical and just demands, he exhorts Alfonso VI of Castile and Leon to relinquish uncatholic additions *(contra catholicam fidem inserta)* to the liturgy and to return to the ancient custom *(prisca consuetudo)* of the Roman Church; and, in a reform decree concerning ember day fasting and ordination times published at the Roman Lenten Synod of 1078, he upholds the old authority *(vetus auctoritas)* of the Fathers against unauthorized new custom *(nova consuetudo aecclesie nulla fulta auctortate).*

A strong link connects both type of antitheses with the compatibility claimed by Gregory in his letters, of lawful and necessary renewal (*renovare, innovare, restaurare, instaurare, corrigere,* etc.) and of avoidance of rash innovation (*nihil novi superinducere, non de nostro sensu exculpere, non nova aut nostra proferre,* etc.).

Thus, in 1075, in a letter addressed to Rudolf of Swabia concerning the recalcitrant German episcopate, he demands renewal and observation of long neglected canon law especially with regard to simony and clerical incontinence. So far detestable uncanonical custom prevails in spite of all admonitions. Under these circumstances, he writes, it is much better to use even new means *(nova consilia)* in restoring what is God's justice than to allow the souls of men to perish together with the neglected laws. Here as elsewhere Gregory makes it clear that reform may on principle include the taking of new measures, the promulgation of new laws; but usually he balances such statements in the sense that, though as Pope he could posit new law, he does not do so, but only reaffirms the old.

In an important letter to Anno of Cologne of March 29, 1075, Gregory explicitly states that the Roman Church may issue new laws against new abuses, but on the other hand equally strongly asserts that the decrees on clerical celibacy published at the famous Lenten Synod of that year, are not his own invention but identical with the canons of the Fathers:

Novit enim fraternitas tua quia precepta hec non de nostro sensu exculpimus, sed antiquorum patrum sanctiones Spiritu Sancto predictante prolatas officii nostri necessitate in medium propalamus . . . quamquam huic sancte Romane ecclesie semper licuit semperque licebit contra noviter increscentes excessus nova quoque decreta atque remedia procurare que rationis et auctoritatis edita iudicio nulli hominum sit fas ut irrita refutare.[10]

On the same day, he writes in the same vein to Wezilo of Magdeburg that he is not proposing his own decrees, even though he would be entitled to do so if it was necessary—rather he is simply renewing ancient canon law:

Non nostra decreta, quamquam licenter si opus esset possemus, vobis proponimus, sed a sanctis patribus statuta renovamus . . .[11]

Toward the end of 1075, Gregory in a well known letter to Henry IV tries to explain to him the intentions of the decree prohibiting lay investiture which had been announced at the Roman Lenten Synod just mentioned. Again he denies that he has invented new things, he only wants to follow the beaten path of the Fathers. The decree against lay investiture, which some all too humanly considered an unbearable burden, he would rather call *truth* and light and a necessity for salvation; but, in order not to upset the king too much through the change of an *evil custom*, the Pope would be willing to apply the decree less strictly wherever the honour of Christ and the salvation of souls are not at stake.

In the following year, in replying to Bishop Henry of Liège's inquiry concerning the cause of Bishop William of Utrecht (then, perhaps, the staunchest anti-Gregorian among the German bishops), he writes that he is only defending the sentences and laws of the Fathers: he does not set forth *nova aut nostra* [new things or our private devices].

One of Gregory's most illuminating statements on Church reform as the vindication of truth against wicked custom is found in his letter to the clergy and people of Aquileia concerning their newly elected patriarch. There, he defines his conception of canonical elections which, he says, is not an invention of his, not a novelty, but in accordance with the doctrine of the Fathers and the Gospels:

Antiqua et nota sacre institutionis est regula, non ab hominibus sed ab Iesu Christo Deo et Domino nostro plenissima sue sapientie consideratione et veritatis diffinitione sancita . . . Quapropter quod in ecclesia diu peccatis facientibus neglectum et nefanda consuetudine corruptum fuit et est, nos ad honorem Dei et salutem totius christianitatis innovare et restaurare cupimus, videlicet ut . . . talis et eo ordine eligatur episcopus qui iuxta veritatis sententiam non fur et latro dici debeat (cf. John 10, 1) . . . Et ideo nichil novi, nichil nostris adinventionibus superinducere conamur, sed illud solummodo querimus quod et omnium salus postulat et necessitas, ut in ordinatione episcoporum secundum communem sanctorum patrum intelligentiam et approbationem primo omnium evangelica et canonica servetur auctoritas.[12]

---

[10] [For your Fraternity knows that we have not carved these precepts out of our own understanding, but that, through the requirement of our office, we publish the sanctions of the ancient Fathers, which were declared through the preaching of the Holy Ghost . . . although this holy Roman Church has always been allowed, and always will be allowed, to enact new decrees and remedies against newly arising excesses, and although it is wrongful for any man to refute as defective such decrees issued according to reason and authority.—Ed.]

Register II, 67, ed. Caspar, pp. 223f.

[11] [We do not set before you our own decrees (although, had there been need of it, we could licitly have done so), but we renew statutes issued by the holy Fathers.—Ed.]

Register II, 68, ed. Caspar, p. 226.

[12] [The rule is ancient and known to be of sacred institution, sanctioned, not by men, but by Jesus

The *veritatis sententia* [sentence of truth] here mentioned, and quoted in full earlier in the same letter, is Christ's saying "He that entereth not by the door into the sheepfold, but climbeth up another way, the same is a thief and a robber, but he that entereth in by the door, is the shepherd of the sheep" (John 10, 1 f.). *Veritas,* therefore, means Christ Himself, and the antithesis of ultimate *veritas* and unjustifiable *consuetudo* in this letter is not unlike the one formulated in JL 5277: "I am the truth, not the custom." While mere custom is either too old or too new, truth is always the same, ever old and ever new. That is why Gregory can act as a reformer and yet disclaim any intention of innovation. The deepest meaning of his idea of reform really is not that of mere innovation; it is renewal of truth which itself is ageless. Reestablished truth is both older and newer [than] intervening "untruthful" custom.

A letter to the Empress Agnes, one of Gregory VII's very personal utterances, lays bare the spiritual foundations upon which be built this conception of a Church reform in which the "old" and the "new" are linked together:

> Per vos itaque novum exemplum antique letitie, per vos, inquam, ille mulieres olim querentes Dominum in monumento sepe nobis ad memoriam redeunt. Nam sicut ille pre cunctis discipulis ad sepulchrum Domini miro caritatis ardore venerunt, ita vos ecclesiam Christi quasi in sepulchro afflictionis positam pre multis immo pene pre omnibus terrarum principibus pio amore visitatis et ut ad statum libertatis sue resurgat totis viribus annitentes quasi angelicis instructe responsis ceteros ad suffragium laborantis ecclesie provocatis.[13]

In Gregory's view then, the tragic figure of Henry IV's mother, bent upon reestablishing and preserving peace between Empire and Papacy, typifies in a new way *(novum exemplum)* the ancient joyfulness *(antiqua letitia)* of the Saviour's victory over death: she renews, as it were, the holy women's visit to the sepulchre of the Lord who in the perspective of a time-transcending present is the afflicted Church and whose resurrection, therefore, is the guarantee of the Church's renewed rise to the state of liberty from which she had fallen.

Christ, God and our Lord, out of the fullest consideration of His wisdom and by the judgment of truth . . . Therefore, we have wished to renew and restore to the honor of God and the welfare of all Christendom what has long been, and is, corrupted by sinning and evil custom: namely [we have wished to bring it about] that a man be elected bishop from this order such as might not be called a "thief and a robber" according to the word of truth (cf. John 10:1). . . . And thus we are striving to intrude nothing new, nothing by our own devisings, but we seek only what the welfare and need of all demands: that, first of all, in the ordination of bishops Gospel and canonical authority be preserved, according to the common understanding and approval of the holy Fathers.—Ed.]

Register V, 5, ed. Caspar, p. 353.

[13] [And so, because of you a new example of ancient joy—because of you, I say, these women who once sought the Lord in the tomb often return to our memory. For just as, with love's wondrous ardor, they went to the Lord's sepulchre before all the disciples, so with pious love do you visit the Church, as one set in the sepulchre of afflictions, before many—indeed before all the princes of the earth. And, as though instructed by angelic replies, striving with all your powers to the end that she may rise again to the state of her liberty, you call forth others to succor the endangered Church.—Ed.]

Register I, 85, ed. Caspar, p. 122.

This letter, in full, in English, in *Correspondence*, *Reg.* VII by Ephraim Emerton, Columbia U. Press, 1932, p.37

KARL F. MORRISON (b.1936) is professor of medieval history at the University of Chicago. He has written extensively on medieval political thought. In addition to *Tradition and Authority in the Western Church, ca. 300–1140* (1969), his works include *The Two Kingdoms: Ecclesiology in Carolingian Political Thought* (1964) and *Rome and the City of God: An Essay on the Constitutional Relatonship of Empire and Church in the Fourth Century.* (1964).*

Karl F. Morrison

Tradition: A Skeleton in the Gregorians' Closet

From the ecclesiological point of view, the issue of relations between Church and Empire was less critical than questions concerning papal responsibility. The conflict between the papacy and temporal rulers could be settled by a straightforward, political engagement; the Concordat of Worms was a pragmatic agreement of that sort. Issues of authority within the Church, however, could be settled only by delicate rationalization, by theoretical explanations that former practice had been erroneous in some degree, though it was commonly judged right, and that it had been corrected by new establishments.

The intellectual terms at issue were legal; the subject of dispute was authority. Perhaps exaggerated by the excitement of conflict, distorted by enthusiasm for personal or partisan interests, or modified in hope of compromise, the views expressed are often without logical order. Many fundamental questions of Church order were not even asked, especially concerning the nature and purpose of law and office, and the proper pattern of institutional relationships. But one issue was plainly drawn: the legal relevance of canons and the degrees of responsibility that they imposed upon each hierarchic rank.

Some thinkers held the view, familiar as early as in the papacy's Byzantine period, that the canons comprised an immutable rule of order binding upon all bishops. Writers thoroughly disciplined in canonistic thought, however, had long understood that canons were not immutable. Despite his insistence that the canons were "eternal," Hincmar of Rheims once acknowledged that they were framed to answer particular requirements, and that they lapsed into desuetude with the passage of time. That seems also to have been the view of Agobard of Lyons and Regino of Prüm, and in the late tenth century Abbo of Fleury expressed it once more. Canons sometimes contradicted each other, Abbo observed, and one synod commanded what another forbade, because the rules of various provinces normally changed according to the influence of geography, historical circumstances, and other necessities.

Pope Victor II stated the Gregorian position when he wrote that the Lord had established the Roman Church over nations and kingdoms, "to root out and destroy and plant and build in His name. Indeed, [He commanded this] so that, as long as His holy Church, spread throughout the whole earth, shall be subject to temporal mutability, and shall alternate in the various and constant changes of waning and waxing, like the moon in its monthly course, it may unceasingly be discerned in the Church what the assiduous husbandman ought to root out or plant and what the wise architect should destroy or build."

Advocates of papal ecclesiology neither resolved nor even seriously raised the critical issue of official responsibility. In their eyes, that question was moot because of the special relationship between Christ and St. Peter and the inherently apostolic character of the papacy, through succession to St. Peter, because of identification of dissent from the Roman Church with heresy and even idolatry, and because of Rome's juridical supremacy.

All reformers understood that popes had great latitude in legal matters. But was the papal authority unlimited? There was no general agreement. The lines of debate were never clearly drawn, but all issues derived from one basic question: How far was the pope bound to observe old laws and to honor old practices? Did the popes have power merely to restore, to lead the Church in some details back to the good, old order, or did they have the greater power to destroy the old root and branch and set up new orders?

What was the Gregorian position? In terms of law, the Gregorians based their reform on the freedom to modify or even to exclude ancient rulings and to create and execute new ones. They declared that the correction of abuses they had undertaken was merely reform, the recovery of an ancient order. Peter Damian knew that the Gospel was in constant danger, and that the base desires even of one schismatic man could overturn the labor of the Apostles and darken the splendor of the universal Church. When a reformer, Gregory VI, acceded to the papacy, after a long series of flagrant simoniacs, Peter wrote to the new Pope rejoicing that the golden age of the Apostles would return through the reflowering of discipline. He found in the lives and precepts of the Fathers since that age a continuation of apostolic teaching which the corruption of his own "iron age" had interrupted. After the Synod of Sutri, he wrote to Henry III in similar terms: "Let the heavens rejoice, therefore, let the earth exult, since truly Christ is known to rule in His King, and now at the very end of time, the golden age of David is renewed." Gregory VII also wrote that he labored to restore the Church to the state of ancient religion, and, in a striking metaphor, he commended the Empress Agnes and Beatrice and Mathilda of Tuscany for their support. "And so, because of you a new example of ancient joy, because of you, I say, these women who once sought the Lord in the tomb often return to our memory. For just as, with love's wondrous ardor, they went to the Lord's sepulchre before all the disciples, so with pious love do you visit the Church, as one set in the sepulchre of afflictions, before many — indeed before all the princes of the earth. And, as though instructed by angelic replies, striving with all your powers to the end that she may rise again to the state of her liberty, you call forth others to succor the endangered Church."

The movement, however, was more than an effort to recover a lost order, to revive the tormented, but fully formed, body of Christ. In their work, the Gregorians advanced a curiously ambivalent view of the past, and particularly of the concept of tradition. Gregory, as well as the reformers who preceded him and those who followed, identified their work with the ancient truth of the Church. Leo IX consciously imitated the customs *(mores)* of Leo I; the popes from the time of Clement II to the conflict between Innocent II and Anacletus II chose their pontifical names from the list of Roman bishops in the apostolic and patristic ages; and all the reformers, including Gregory VII, steadfastly maintained that they were not introducing new doctrines and observances, but only restoring the doctrine of the Fathers.

Yet none of the canonistic anthologies of the period contains a specific entry or cluster of entries concerning tradition, and, despite its importance for twelfth-century polemicists, the word "tradition" itself rarely occurs in the Gregorians' letters.

In dealing with other churches, the reform leaders militantly opposed ancient forms and usages. They refused to acknowledge as legitimate the extraordinary diversities which separated believers. For them, the unity of faith and universality of the Church were largely synonymous, and the factors which had divided Christendom must be dismissed as conducive to schism and replaced by Roman norms. By the end of the period under review, Rome had first allowed, and then forbidden, the use of vernacular languages in the Divine Office, commanded Milanese, Armenian, and Spanish prelates to replace their own rites with the Roman, and declared that those who did not adhere to Roman disciplinary practices (such as the enforcement of clerical celibacy) were outside the Church. Rome was seeking by spontaneous administrative action to establish the Church as an institution, and to supply the uniformity of language, discipline, and creed necessary to that plan.

Other comments of the reformers concerning Rome itself reveal a settled contempt for antiquity unrecommended by other qualifications. A fragmentary letter attributed to Gregory VII quotes with approval the comment of St. Cyprian that the Lord did not say, "I am custom," but "I am truth," and that any custom, however old or widespread, must be subordinated to truth and discarded if it ran contrary to truth. Together with the Gregorians' assertions of papal supremacy, the Cyprianic passage epitomized the thought of an early reformer, perhaps Humbert of Silva Candida, who wrote that the Roman See commanded such respect that all men sought the discipline of the holy canons and the ancient institution of the Christian religion from the mouth of its governor *(presessoris)* rather than from holy writings and the traditions of the Fathers. Gregory once wrote that the Fathers had corrected the negligence of the primitive Church; in his own reforms, he undertook what he clearly considered a similar breach with received conventions, a selective rejection of the teachings and practices of the immediate past.

It was paradoxical that the Gregorians adopted as their own the sentence which St. Cyprian wrote against a bishop of Rome, that they rejected immediately received conventions and, at the same time, claimed sanctions of antiquity for their work. This ambivalence was resolved according to the Gregorians' thought by a doctrine of unlimited papal discretion in legal matters. Only Rome could distinguish between ancient error and truth, suspend the force of just canons in need, or promulgate new laws to meet unprecedented necessity. The antiquity of Roman discretionary powers was, in the last analysis, the only rule of antiquity which the reformers unreservedly accepted.

The first reformer pope owed his pontifical accession to uncanonical procedure; his successors defended him by arguing that the normal force of the canons had been voided by necessity. Throughout the period under review, there were thinkers who argued more generally that the canons were not in any case binding upon Roman bishops. As Bernald wrote, "For no pope deprives his successor of the privilege of the Apostolic See to mitigate, according to the the necessity of his time, not only the canons but also the sanctions of his predecessor. In this he does not repudiate his predecessor, since he knows that his own establishments may sometime be mitigated."

Gregorians considered temporal law external to the law of the Church. An imperialist writer, Petrus Crassus, wrote that God established two kinds of law: assigning one to clergy, through the apostles and their successors, and the other to laymen, through emperors and kings. Each law benefited the other, however; and the Church used both bodies of law. The reformers, however, were concerned to draw the line of legal relevance sharply. Though they may have lacked full knowledge of Roman law, their familiarity with it was sufficiently detailed to persuade them that no regulation of Roman law could be invoked in ecclesiastical cases unless it accorded with the canons. A very similar position led Hildebrand to argue, in 1059, that a decree of Louis the Pious on canons regular was invalid. Louis, he said, had no right to change the "apostolic rule . . . without the authority and consent of the Holy Roman and Apostolic See; for although an emperor and a devout man, he was a layman. But neither could any bishop do that, for it is not their part to introduce a new rule into the churches by their office or judgment alone, especially a rule contrary to [the Roman See]. . . ." Deusdedit argued on broader grounds, but to the same end, that the foundation of the faith stood in the patriarchal sees, particularly in Rome, Alexandria, and Antioch. If one of the three fell, two would stand; if two fell, the faith of the Roman patriarch would never fail. Secular powers had no share in this structure. "For God is read to have spoken to pontiffs, not to emperors, 'Who hears you, hears me, and whoever spurns you, spurns me,' etc. And again, 'Whatever you shall bind on earth will be bound also in heaven,' etc." Therefore temporal rulers had no power to change "the Church's tradition, established by God," for, as Gelasius I had written, God wished the clergy to be ordered not by civil laws and worldly powers, but by pontiffs and priests. Secular laws could be invoked only if they did not contradict ecclesiastical sanctions. Indeed, priests took precedence over kings in the promulgation of laws, for God first established His laws for kings and other believers through the agency of priests.

Consequently, when they wrote of ecclesiastical law, the reformers thought chiefly of the canons of synods and councils and of papal decretals, "the venerable councils of holy Fathers and the precepts of the Apostles, and of apostolic men." Upon these documents they exercised their very keen powers of historical and textual criticism; from them, and especially from the canons of the synods they themselves held, they sought to justify their tightening of ecclesiastical discipline. In that body of laws, if anywhere, lay restraints on papal discretion.

Perhaps the most influential and extreme summary of the Gregorians' view on law occurs in the letters of Gregory VII. Though far less refined a canonist than Peter Damian, Anselm of Lucca, or Deusdedit, Gregory possessed a sound knowledge of the canons, and his decretals were the chief instruments by which the reformers' legal program was enacted. Gregory wrote once that "the image of God is the form of justice," and he generally identified contempt for law, collapse of order, and schism from the true faith. Sacrilege and rapine enfeebled France because the laws were neglected and justice was utterly crushed. Likewise, disorders in the Church occurred precisely because wicked men had striven to overturn the decrees of the Fathers and, with them, orthodox belief. Gregory's letters indeed are characterized by insistence that violators of "Christian law" *(lex christiana)* or the "law of Christ" *(lex Christi)* be punished, that canonical order be preserved, and that priests and bishops obey God rather than the princes and potentates of this world, diligently honoring the law of their Creator and preferring to sacrifice

their lives rather than justice. Priests who infringed the law of God, the rules established by the holy Fathers through the inspiration of the Holy Ghost, denied the faith.

The law on which the preservation of the faith depended was in part an unwritten moral law. But, in its positive aspects, it was a law moderated by papal discretion. In his decrees, Gregory often maintained that he was not establishing new regulations, but merely renewing the rules of the Fathers. His hierarchic policies showed the same character. He attempted, for example, to establish his direct ecclesiastical headship by sending legates, a practice which some Bohemians repudiated as an innovation, but which Gregory defended as merely the restoration of a practice which the negligence of his predecessors and other bishops had interrupted. His office compelled him, he wrote, to keep vigilant watch over all churches to see that they rightly held the "documents of the faith and the holy rules of Scripture," for to subvert the canons was to rend the unity of Christ's body. Yet the Dictatus Papae asserted that only the pope might "establish new laws according to the need of the time," and that no chapter or book could be considered canonical without his approval. And Gregory's letters reiterate that the Roman Church "has always been and will always be permitted to provide new decrees and remedies against newly arisen aberrations," that those new decrees were indisputably binding, and that Rome likewise had the power "to tolerate some things, even to conceal some things, following the temperance of discretion rather than the rigor of the canons." He used this discretion most notably in making allowances for bishops who had unwittingly violated his own decree against lay investiture, due to its novelty, though in a letter to Henry

IV he wrote that he had in that decree resorted to the decrees and teaching of the Fathers and "established nothing new, nothing by our own invention." Rather, he declared, men must cast aside their error and follow "the first and only rule of ecclesiastical discipline and the narrow way of the saints." A similar ambivalence appears in his concept of ecclesiastical privilege. Some allegations to the contrary, he declared that privileges were granted according to circumstances of person, time, and place, as necessity or utility required, that they could subsequently be changed subject to the "authority of the holy Fathers," and that even privileges established by popes could be overturned, if it could be shown that the issuing pontiffs had been deceived into acting contrary to the establishments of the Fathers.

For Gregory, and for the other reformers whose position he represented, ecclesiastical law was a constantly developing body of regulations, the components of which were established by bishops—singly, in their individual letters and treatises, or collectively, in their synodal decrees. The Roman Church held general supervision over the administration of law, and in their decretals bishops of Rome added to the body of law according to necessity. Their attitude toward antiquity as a legal sanction was ambivalent, but, on balance, they subordinated it to the general rule of papal discretion. Gregory VII wrote that the "law of Roman pontiffs" had prevailed in more lands than the law of Roman emperors.

This characteristic of general applicability followed naturally from the argument, common among papal thinkers, that decrees of Roman bishops were normative among legal sources, and that the canonicity of a given text depended upon its presumed concordance with, or explicit approval by, papal decretals.

Against doctrines which tended to curtail their powers, papal writers advanced with ever-greater refinement the doctrine that the Roman See was the epitome of the universal Church, and that the pope epitomized the Roman See. The reformers of the early twelfth century, no less than their predecessors, resolutely argued that their work honored the ancient traditions and decrees of the Fathers and the Apostles. Still, the emphasis upon papal discretion which led the early Gregorians to an ambivalent view of tradition operated also among their successors.

Like earlier reformers, papal thinkers recalled that Christ said not "I am custom," but "I am truth." More clearly than his immediate predecessors, Innocent II exposed the hierarchic implications of that distinction. Innocent wrote that no dishonesty or change of circumstance should upset or disturb what the holy Fathers instituted; he professed to uphold the decrees of the sacred canons and the general custom of the Church. Indeed, he said, the essential character of the priesthood itself was fidelity to the establishments of the Fathers: the priest ignorant of the law was no priest, for the priest's function was to know the law and to answer questions concerning the law. Still, though he once inveighed against "new laws and customs," he admitted on another occasion the "most recent establishments of councils" together with decrees of the Fathers and ancient conciliar decrees as authoritative. For Innocent, the criterion between "custom" and "truth," the reconciling factor between ancient law and authentic change, was the hierarchic supremacy of Rome, particularly as expressed in adjudication. "According to the custom of the ancients," St. Peter and his successors established bishops, archbishops, and primates in appropriate sees to teach the divine law to the people. The holy Fathers wished diverse ranks and orders to be in the Church so that, through subjection and reverence of lesser officers to greater, one unifying bond would prevail over diversity and the administration of each office would be rightly discharged. In this order, Rome was the "head and hinge" *(caput et cardo)*, the "mother" of the office held by all bishops. The Lord established St. Peter His vicar and the master of all the Church. Consequently, the Apostolic See could receive appeal from any part of the Church; and Innocent bitterly denounced attempts to curtail that power in its broadest construction as presumption against the canons and blasphemy against the Holy Ghost. Innocent indeed wrote that charity bound the orders in the Church together and produced the reverence of the lesser toward the greater officers. But the effective manifestation of charity was obedience, especially to the privilege of St. Peter, juridically conceived; for that was the sum of the Church's law, the safeguard of ancient establishments, and the assurance of authentic change.

Tradition conveyed principally faith and practices; order was foremost in the Gregorians' minds. Tradition had required either stability or the constant historical elaboration of a deposit of doctrine. The Gregorians argued for expedience. As Gregory VII wrote, the primitive Church dissembled some things until the age of the Fathers, when they were set right, and the normal practice of the Roman Church was to relax canonical regulations or to conceal some things entirely, according to the need of the time. Sudden change, or innovation, which the apologists and Fathers feared, was thus accommodated in the reformers' thought. Indeed, it became a normal instrument of hierarchic government. Tradition had been general to all believers. The Gregorians were ambivalent toward tradition when they did not simply ignore it, for they defined cohesion within the Church in terms of obedience to papal decrees. Tradition was, at best, a skeleton in their closet, a potential threat to their doctrine of full discretion.

After the death of Gregory VII (1085), the Investiture Controversy continued for nearly forty years, An astonishing interlude came in the pontificate of Paschal II. As the hostile imperial army marched toward Rome in 1110, the Pope engaged in urgent negotiations with King Henry V, who was demanding that Paschal crown him as emperor. Paschal could see only one basis of compromise, and that a radical one. He would both reject the principle of lay investiture, and destroy the basis of the actual practice by renouncing the feudal lands and services that tied churches to secular control. In bargaining with Henry, he had been led to expect that the King would respond by giving up the right of lay investiture, and that the two acts—his and Henry's—would end both the practice and the dispute. He was deceived. Read in St. Peter's as the coronation ceremony got under way, the Pope's text, or *privilegium*, was shouted down by the bishops attending. Probably according to plan, Henry used the disorder as an excuse to break off the coronation rites and to take Paschal into protective custody. In virtual imprisonment, the Pope was induced to issue another *privilegium*, confirming lay investiture. This act reversed the whole reform program begun under Pope Leo IX and championed to the death by Gregory VII and Urban II. The reformers believed that Paschal had betrayed them, and they compared the *privilegia*—which they considered depraved and called *pravilegia*—with Judas' betrayal of Christ. Though he renounced the decrees after Henry released him, Paschal labored under this reproach until his death.*

Text

Paschal II's Privilegia *in Favor of Henry V (1111)*

The First *Privilegium*

Paschal, bishop, servant of the servants of God, to [our] beloved son Henry, and to his successors in perpetuity.

It is both forbidden by the institution of divine law and interdicted by the holy canons that priests be occupied in worldly cares, and that they go to the civil court except to free the condemned or for the

---

*From *Monumenta Germaniae Historica, Constitutiones*, vol. 1 (Hannover, 1893), pp. 141ff, 144ff. Translated by Karl F. Morrison.

sakes of others who suffer injustice. Wherefore the Apostle Paul says, "If you have secular judgments, establish those who have little esteem in the Church to judge."

But in parts of your kingdom, bishops and abbots are so much occupied with worldly cares that they are forced to frequent the civil court assiduously and to lead troops. These things, indeed, are hardly or never occasioned without acts of rapine, sacrilege, arson, or murder. For the ministers of the altar have been made ministers of the court, because they have accepted from kings cities, duchies, marks, rights of coinage, manors and the like pertaining to the service of the kingdom. Wherefore also the intolerable practice has grown upon the Church that bishops-elect in no way accept consecration without first being invested by the royal hand. From this cause, both the madness of simoniac heresy and, sometimes, very great ambition has brought about the invasion of episcopal sees without any election. Occasionally, intruders have even been invested while the bishops were still alive.

Aroused by these and many other evils, which were commonly related through investiture, our predecessors, Gregory VII and Urban II, pontiffs of happy memory, condemned those investitures at lay hands, having often assembled episcopal councils on the matter, and judged that those who had obtained churches through lay investitures must be deposed, and that the donors must be deprived of communion according to that chapter of the Apostolic Canons which runs as follows: "If any bishop having used the powers of this world obtains a church by means of them, let him be deposed and sequestered, and all who communicate with him." Following their footsteps, we also have confirmed their sentence in episcopal council.

To you therefore, dearest son Henry, King—and now, through our office by the grace of God Emperor of the Romans— we command that all those regalia be relinquished to the kingdom which manifestly belonged to the kingdom in the time of Charles, Louis, Henry, and your other predecessors. We also interdict and forbid under sentence of anathema that any bishop or abbot, present or future, usurp those same regalia, to wit: cities, duchies, marks, counties, rights of coinage, rights of toll, rights of market, advowsons of the kingdom, rights of hundred-men, and manors which were manifestly of the kingdom, with their appurtenances, militia, and castles of the kingdom. Nor may they henceforth involve themselves in these regalia except by the king's grace. Moreover, it is not allowed to our successors, who follow after us in the Apostolic See, to disquiet you or the kingdom on this matter.

Further, we judge that the churches with oblations and hereditary possessions which manifestly do not belong to the kingdom are to remain free, as on the day of your coronation you promised to the omnipotent Lord in the sight of the whole Church. For it behooves bishops freed from worldly cares to exercise care of their peoples and not to be absent any longer from their churches. For, according to the Apostle Paul, they keep watch, as they are to give account for their peoples' souls.

The Second *Privilegium*

Paschal, bishop, servant of the servants of God, to [our] dearest son in Christ, Henry, glorious King of the Germans, and through the grace of omnipotent God, Emperor Augustus of the Romans: greeting and apostolic benediction.

Divine disposition has established that your kingdom is connected in a singular way to the holy Roman church, inasmuch as, with the grace of probity and prudence, your predecessors have acceded to the crown and empire of the Roman City. Indeed, through the ministry of our priesthood, divine majesty has advanced your person also, dearest son Henry, to the office of its crown and empire. Therefore, that prerogative of office which our predecessors have conceded to your predecessors, the catholic emperors, and confirmed in the texts of privileges, we also concede to Your Love and confirm with the text of the present privilege: that you confer investiture of crozier and ring on the bishops and abbots of your kingdom, elected freely without violence and simony. But after investiture, let them canonically receive consecration from the bishop under whose jurisdiction they belong. If, however, someone is elected by clergy and people without your assent, unless he be invested by you, let him not be consecrated, except, of course, those who by custom stand under the disposition of archbishops or the Roman pontiff. Naturally, the archbishops or bishops may have the freedom

to consecrate canonically bishops and abbots invested by you. For your predecessors enriched the churches of their kingdom with such great benefices of their regalia that it is right for that kingdom to be fortified especially with the troops of bishops and abbots, and for the popular dissentions which often occur in elections to be settled by the royal majesty.

For this reason, Your Prudence and Power ought to take special care that the greatness of the Roman church and the welfare of other churches be preserved, with the Lord's assistance, through your benefices and services.

If, finally, any ecclesiastical or secular person, knowing this text of our concession, dares to go against it with bold affrontery, may he be fettered with the bond of anathema unless he repent, and may he suffer loss of honor and office. May divine mercy, however, guard those who observe this decree and grant that your person and power rule happily to its own honor and glory.

In a reminiscent mood, after he had achieved fame as the historian of medieval Rome, FERDINAND GREGOROVIUS (1821–1891) ascribed his interest in the Middle Ages, and the liberal views by which he judged historical figures and events, to two influences. The first was the fact that he had lived as a child in the castle of the Teutonic Knights at Neidenburg, East Prussia. The second was Russia's bloody repression of the Polish revolution in 1830, which he witnessed personally as a boy of nine. It would be fair to add a third element, the strict Lutheranism of Gregorovius's father, which not only gave the dominant tone to his childhood but also led him, at parental insistence, to take a degree in theology from the University of Königsberg (1841). After some years as a private tutor and a spare-time poet and novelist of the most heavily romantic cast, Gregorovius went to Rome, where he spent more than twenty years (1852–1874). There he completed all his major works, including his *History of the City of Rome in the Middle Ages (1896)*. He never accepted an academic appointment. The following selection shows clearly the impact of the stormy political life that Gregorovius actually saw in Rome on his assessment of the past.*

Ferdinand Gregorovius

Recovery of Apostolic Ideals

[*On Henry V's entrance into Italy, 1110*] What could the Pope expect from a young prince who had inherited the craft of the father whom he had over-reached, and who, endowed with far greater energy, was resolved to prosecute the same struggle for the rights of the crown which the fate of Henry IV had clearly shown to be the condition necessary to the continued existence of the empire? Henry V approached, as his envoys at Chalons had already threatened, to assert the right of investiture with the sword, and to demolish Hildebrand's audacious structure. The position of Paschalis II was more difficult than that of Gregory had been, for the Normans were crippled by enervation and fear. Matilda was old, and remained neutral; religious passions, formerly such powerful allies

*From Ferdinand Gregorovius, *History of the City of Rome in the Middle Ages* translated by Annie Hamilton (London: George Bell, 1896), vol. 4, pt. 2, pp. 330–337. Footnotes omitted.

of the hierarchy, had cooled, and Christendom demanded the settlement of the dispute at almost any cost.

Henry wrote to the Romans from Arezzo that, hitherto prevented from doing honour to the capital of his empire, he was now approaching, and he demanded that envoys should be sent to meet him. His ambassadors went to Rome to make arrangements for the coronation, and met Pier Leone, the plenipotentiary of the Pope, in S. Maria in Turri. The coronation was to be the final act of a treaty, but difficulty was experienced in framing this—the first of all concordats. Henry was obliged to insist on the right of investiture which all his predecessors had exercised; the Pope was obliged to take his stand on the decrees of his predecessors, which forbade investiture by lay hands, and to which he had himself given his solemn ratification. Could the King surrender to the Pope the sole right of appointing bishops, when these bishops received principalities as fiefs from the empire? If these powerful bishops and abbots were entirely severed from the State, and became vassals solely of the Roman Church, would not their power become illimitable, and would they not, as Gregory VII desired, swallow up the State? The consequences of the royal investiture were, on the other hand, ruinous to the Church; the Church remained the vassal of the crown. But this evil, which was undeniable, might be removed as soon as the bishops renounced the temporal power and all political position.

The question of investiture was, at this time, as difficult as the question of the continued existence of the Dominium Temporale of the popes, the last remains of the mediaeval body of the Church, has become to-day within a united Italy. In both questions we find the same interconnection of things, moral and political; both consequently, like a Gordian knot, were first cut by the sword. It will ever remain worthy of remark that a pope of the twelfth century advanced, with lofty resolution, a principle, the realisation of which would have invested the Church with a higher moral power, a principle, however, which was too ethereal for a time when the law of might prevailed. Paschalis II recognised the right of the crown, a right which was as clear as the sun; he admitted that, after it had surrendered such immense revenues to the churches, the empire could not exist without the privilege of investiture. As the young and faithless son of Henry IV approached Rome with a formidable army, leaving ruined cities in his rear, he may have appeared to the trembling Pope like some beast of prey, whose ferocity might be appeased by booty. In his direst need, and in order that he might save her life and her freedom, the Pope threw him the possessions of the Church. He proposed that the bishops should restore all their crown property to the empire, and live henceforward on tithes; that the King should permanently renounce the right of investiture, and should consequently, in exchange, bestow the priceless gift of freedom from the State upon the Church. Had Paschalis II been able to realise this pure and apostolic idea, he would have proved himself a greater man than Gregory VII, and the true reformer among the popes. The judgment of a virtuous and unworldly monk was forced to recognise that the corruption of the clergy and the slavery of the Church were merely the consequences of her unapostolic secularisation; Paschalis, however, did not show himself a man of so great a mind that we can venture to ascribe his scheme to a bold desire for reform; it was, on the contrary, rather the suggestion of despair. The twelfth century was not ripe for the premature idea of the emancipation of the Church. The sacred institution, which should have been merely the incorporeal kingdom of light, of love, and of virtue, continued to be obscured by earthly vapours, like a misty sun, whose rays, had they pierced in all their purity, would perhaps have worked without effect, or even with destruction, on the savagery of semi-barbarous times. The feudal interconnection of secular and spiritual power weighed for centuries upon society, and not until the sixteenth century did the idea of Paschalis (which in him was probably only due to a naïve simplicity) attain a mature and powerful consciousness.

To the clergy, accustomed to power and splendour, his proposal must have appeared one of unequalled renunciation: the prelates were called on to surrender immense estates, cities, taxes, rights of market and coinage, justice, and the authority of margraves. Nevertheless they would not have become poor as the apostles, since each bishopric still possessed its private estate, and even tithes and offerings still remained a lucrative source of wealth. But with the loss of princely power the bishops became defenceless against the political power; they were robbed of their influence in the world, which only respects the power that gives and takes, and that can inspire fear by magnificence. Every bishop would have refused to renounce the illustrious position of Member of the imperial Parliament, in order to become a free and virtuous but insignificant servant of the Lord, and all would have been able to reproach Paschalis for having acted disinterestedly at the cost of others, when he himself, the Pope, never contemplated the renunciation of the sceptre of the ecclesiastical State. On the contrary, he expressly stipulated beforehand that Henry should restore this State according to the limits of the ancient donations. If worldly splendour were unseemly in bishops, was it not equally unseemly in the Pope? If it were unbecoming in an abbot to mount his warhorse in coat of mail and ride at the head of his vassals, must not the sight of the Holy Father in the field of battle have been still more at variance with the principles of Christianity? The possession of crown fiefs involved the bishops in constant traffic with the world, but what for centuries had been the history of the Roman ecclesiastical State? At the same time, the existence of such a State, even in so miserable a form, was now an essential condition for the spiritual independence of the Pope. The fatal irony which was attached to its principle made the Dominium Temporale at the same time the shield and the Achilles' heel of the Pope, made him simultaneously a king and a martyr, the exiled possessor of an estate. The dust of the little, ever-rebellious clod of Rome hung to the feet of the high priest of Christianity with sufficient weight to prevent him from soaring to too lofty regions, where, as an almost divine being, he would have been removed beyond the ideas of his time, or as a tyrant of the moral world, inaccessible to secular hands, would have withdrawn himself beyond reach of their demands. Paschalis scarcely asked himself the question whether the union of priest and king in his own person was beneficial; and if a malicious bishop had expressed doubts as to the principles on which the State of Peter was founded, he would have replied with the more reason what Pius IX replied to the theoretical and practical usurpers of the Temporal Dominion in the present day, merely that the provinces of S. Peter were not fiefs of the empire. When in 1862 one of the most memorable of revolutions overthrew the ancient and decayed State of the Church, it was interesting to reflect that the recognition of the renunciation, which Paschalis so vainly required of the bishops, would have further entailed the suppression of the papal State. And we have just cause for surprise in the fact that, 700 years after Paschalis, this ancient question was discussed with the like fervour by the whole of Europe.

Had Henry V accepted the proposal of the Pope he would immediately have doubled the wealth of the crown; an avaricious monarch would have hastily stretched forth his hand, a more prudent one would have hesitated. The renunciation of the right of investiture involved the loss of all royal influence on the Church, the greatest power of the world at that time. The estates annexed would necessarily have been bestowed as fiefs on others, and would have contributed to increase the power of hereditary nobles; the cities, which were only loosely allied with the bishoprics, would have acquired complete independence. But above all, could Henry believe that bishops and princes would have acquiesced in the proposal of the Pope? Could he believe that it was possible to confiscate so many estates, which a thousand vassals held as fiefs from the crown, without causing an inevitable revolution of the relations of property?

Henry sincerely longed for peace with the Church; he accepted the treaty; but did not reckon on the possibility of its execution.

PETER R. McKEON (b. 1938) is engaged in a study of
the history of medieval councils. The essay reproduced
here is a fine example of how study of canonistic
texts, coupled with common sense, can illuminate
the issues in a diplomatic power play. McKeon teaches
at the University of Illinois, Chicago Circle Campus.*

Peter R. McKeon

Papal Weakness

The investiture controversy has been
the subject of much study by historians
both of the church and of political theory.
Indeed, the period abounds in material
for both branches of endeavor, and no
aspect of it is richer or offers clearer evidence of the close connection which exists
between the development of events and
theory than the actions which followed
granting the privilege of investiture to
Henry V in 1111, which gave the anti-
imperial faction the basis for an onslaught
against the pope and the emperor novel
in nature if not so in intensity, springing
as it did from principles inherent in the
canonist doctrines of the preceding half-
century. It is readily apparent that the
polemic of the years 1111–1112 furnished
in prototype many ideas which would
later find a place in the arguments of advocates of Conciliarism, but sufficient
attention has not yet been given to the
events which underlay this polemic. The
purpose of this paper is to re-examine
these arguments in the context of the
events which followed the Concordat of
Sutri, and in particular to clarify the very
ambiguous circumstances surrounding
the calling and activities of the Lateran
council of 1112 and the equally obscured
reaction of the French episcopacy to this
council, and thus to restore these very
important events, too often glossed over
like inexplicable phenomena in an other-

*Peter R. McKeon, "The Lateran Council of 1112, the 'Heresy' of Lay Investiture, and the Excommunica-
tion of Henry V," *Medievalia et Humanistica*, 17 (1966), pp. 3–12. Footnotes omitted.

wise clearly defined historical development, to the place and proper context which their significance warrants.

In the year 1110 Henry of Germany, free for a time from the strife which had for so many years characterized the government of the empire, led an army into the Italian peninsula, bound for Rome and determined upon the assumption of those supposed rights which the past forty years had rendered so tenuous. The solidification of Henry's rule was in large measure dependent upon his reception by Pope Paschal II. Successor to Urban II, and in the years following his accession an unyielding proponent of his predecessor's aims, Paschal lacked both the statesmanship and the power of the men who had thus far espoused the papal cause. In the hope of real reconciliation the tactics of Guastalla were set aside, and in Sutri on the ninth of February, 1111, the proposal tendered by the pope some five days earlier was confirmed by the German king. The lay power was to renounce all rights to ecclesiastical investiture, and the church in turn to resign possession of all *regalia* [regalian rights].

The publication of this agreement in Rome on 12 February not unsurprisingly raised a storm of protest from all present who had more worldly ambitions than did the pope. Without considering the ideological justifications for Paschal's agreement or the degree of Henry's understanding of its present impracticability, one may note that turmoil followed the reading of the compact. Henry, taking matters into his own hands, after a bloody battle with the Romans absconded with the pope and a number of his retinue. In a period of two months confinement the royal pressure proved too much. The plans of the past February, as well as the program of his more formidable predecessors, were ignored, and on 11 April the pope and some sixteen associates renounced all objections to imperial investiture; free episcopal elections were to be guaranteed, but no election was to be valid unless followed by investiture by the emperor, while this in turn was a necessary prerequisite for any consecration. Henry, now possessing the imperial crown, returned immediately to Germany, leaving the pope free indeed, but sadly shorn of all respect, and open to the attacks of other opponents no less relentless and strong-willed than was the emperor.

The signing of the *privilegium* gave rise immediately to a new wave of reaction. By June of 1111 the bishops opposing any concessions to Henry, taking advantage of the withdrawal of both emperor and pope from Rome, held a sort of *conciliabulum* [caucus] in which the agreement of April was severely criticized. Leaders of this early movement included not only Italian bishops, but also Galo of St-Pol de Léon, the bishop of Paris. But perhaps the most outspoken disapproval came from Bruno of Segni. Writing to Peter of Porto, one of the signers of the *privilegium,* Bruno condemned any support of that agreement, noting that many councils had rejected lay investiture as heretical, and that hence any who took the side of Henry rejected the real church. To Bruno, the nature of the true doctrine was long since clearly defined, and Henry's deviation from these principles made him a heretic whom the pope must disclaim. But, he advises several bishops, the pope's failure to stand firm by the doctrines of his predecessors renders him too suspect, for the truth remains the same, and anyone who takes a stand against this truth is an enemy; there is no middle ground.

Paschal seems to have been quick to see the danger presented to his program by Bruno, and sought to handle this by removal of its source. Informing the bishop, who was also abbot of the monastery of Monte Cassino, that the two offices could not be held simultaneously, the pope ordered Bruno to relinquish the latter, and informed the brothers that they were no longer bound to their old abbot, and should elect a new one. Paschal seems also to have encouraged the Segnese to replace Bruno in his episcopal office, but he failed in this attempt to remove his opponent from all official capacity. The *Chronica Casinensis* gives what may be a quite candid report of Paschal's concern at this time, in quoting a statement ostensibly made by the pope in reference to Bruno: "Si non acceleravero tollere ei abbatiam, futurum est, ut ipse suis argumentationibus Romanum michi tollat pontificatum." [If I don't take his abbacy away from him in a hurry, he, with his arguments, will strip me of the Roman pontificate.]

But spokesmen were not hard to find who would develop and enunciate the principles, both stated and implicit, put forth by the bishop of Segni. Placidius of Nonantula, similarly receiving a defense of the April privilege, responded with a work entitled *Liber de honore ecclesiae* [Book on the Honor of the Church]. He does not challenge, he says, the statement that the pope may alter the laws of the church, but all such alteration must accord with the principles of the holy fathers. But lay investiture, by subjecting the church to the lay power, destroys the freedom which is an essential material of the ecclesiastical edifice. Thus the practice of lay investiture is heretical; the fact that it has become so only recently does not affect this status, and the councils of Gregory VII and Urban II, which condemned this heresy, acted most justly and enacted salutary legislation which cannot be rescinded. Those who would

do so must be called to public investigation, that this error may not spread. And this must apply to all, for the doctrine that "non est discipulus super magistrum" [the disciple is not above the master] is not intended to give unwarranted honor to men, but rather to affirm the honor of God by insuring the safety of his church. In such a matter of faith, the only answer is a council where, as at Nicaea, the priests, and they alone, shall give judgment.

In the face of such opposition Paschal's new resolve quickly withered. Quite possibly intending to give up the papacy, he left Rome suddenly for Pontins, but soon returned. On 26 October he informed the emperor that fear of grave disturbances led him to resign judgment of the present circumstances to God. Thoughts of abdication past, he now issued a call for a general council to meet in the following March.

What had happened to cause this about-face? The paucity of sources and the strong feelings of those contemporaries who have left records makes it difficult to reconstruct the sequence of events and causes, but certain conclusions may be drawn. In the north, as in Italy, the announcement of the *privilegium* had brought about a flurry of invective. Godfrey of Vendôme, at some time in 1111, had sent a strong protest to the pope. The concession of lay investiture, which would undoubtedly lead to the death of the church, must be immediately rescinded. There can be no question of the heretical nature of such interference, which all true catholics must fight with all their strength, and indeed a pastor who goes beyond the faith is no pastor at all, but truly an enemy. More dangerous still to Paschal, Josserand, the archbishop of Lyon, was led by similar beliefs to call his own council in the latter part of 1111, noting in response to the objections voiced by Ivo of Chartres that the pope did not receive an exemption from judgment greater than that of any other bishop. The immediate end of a situation fraught with danger for all the faithful is the matter of primary importance, and Josserand bemoans the condition of a ship, the captain of which, capable in calm weather, is unable to guide his ship during a storm.

There was indeed in France a strong and vocal party which counseled moderation. Ivo of Chartres, as spokesman for the Senonese prelates who refused to attend the synod at Anse, wrote to Josserand in these terms. Lay investiture, he says, is not in itself a heresy, since it is not an error of faith; the heretical aspect, where such exists, proceeds from the diabolic presumption of a layman who attempts to give spiritual investiture. Further, the pope is not to be judged by anyone. An unjust sentence may fail to be executed by the lesser prelates, but the author of such an error cannot rightly be attacked, and in his weakness under stress merits sympathy rather than rebellion. At any rate, notes Ivo, the pope had now decided to reaffirm the decisions of his predecessors, and will thus make clear that the privilege given to Henry V proceeded not from will but from the exigencies of the times.

The outcry in France was not greater in extent or intensity than was that of the Italian prelates. But in France there entered a new element. Louis VI, always eager to maintain the royal hold over the French clergy, now indeed was motivated as well by fear of imperial solidification, and perhaps saw in the current dissension the possibility of himself replacing the emperor as a "patron" of the papacy. At any rate, the French king unobtrusively supported the protests of the radical group against Paschal, and may have been behind the calling of the council at Anse.

Recognition of this fact is vital to the explanation of Paschal's sudden return to Rome, and basic to an understanding of the whole nature of the Lateran council of March 1112. The Italian bishops, however antagonistic to the pope, did not see the substitution of a French tutelage as any answer to their problems or ambitions. But the papal flight opened the way for the French reaction, which must now be countered by a new assertion, and one proceeding from Paschal himself. Thus the pope was returned to Rome, and the call issued for a council at which the pope would "iusserat iussit [et] prohibuerat prohibuit." [He has commanded what he had commanded [and] he has forbidden what he had forbidden.]

Few events in ecclesiastical history of comparable importance to this council, and receiving a similar amount of attention in the works of contemporaries, are so shrouded in the mists of ambiguity. All records of the first four days of this assembly, which met during the week of 18 to 24 March, are missing, while reports of the decisions concerning lay investiture fall into two groups in many respects diametrically opposed. On the one hand, we are told that the pope, while desiring to state his agreement with the doctrines of the predecessors, yet hesitated to because of his prior agreement with the emperor. Finally, after much fruitless discussion, the plan proposed by bishop Gerard of Angoulême, that lay investiture be condemned and the *privilegium* nullified, but the emperor himself not be subject of any excommunication, was adopted by universal acclamation. But other sources insist that by conciliar decree the *privilegium* was declared null and the emperor anathematized as well.

In support of this position it must be noted that among the signers of the decrees are to be found some of the most violent opponents of lay investiture and imperial prerogative, including Bruno of Segni. How can this dilemma be resolved? A possible clue is found in the letter written to Henry in May or June 1112 by Beraldus, the abbot of Farfa. Here Paschal is quoted as having stated "ego non praedico—nec dampno vel excommunico quemquam—nisi quem pater meus Urbanus et Gregorius instituerunt." [I do not preach—nor do I condemn or excommunicate anyone—unless my father Urban, and Gregory, marked him out.] Read in the context of the proposal of Gerard of Angoulême, this statement would specifically spare the emperor (and necessarily thus prevent any decision as to the heretical nature of lay investiture), since Henry V had never been condemned by Urban or Gregory. But taken, on the other hand, as part of Paschal's own pledge of faith, ". . . quod dampnaverunt dampnavimus, quod firmaverunt firmavimus, quod statuerunt statuimus . . . ," [. . . what they had condemned, we have condemned; what they had confirmed, we have confirmed, what they had established, we have established. . . .] it clearly implied the heretical character of lay investiture, and thus the excommunication of the emperor.

What reasons can be assigned for this extraordinary decree? The French dissensions of late 1111 were a very immediate danger not only to the pope, but also to the enunciators of Roman policy who, standing autonomous, might indeed be among the first to promote the deposition of the pope. But the implementation of French protest by lay interest and power changed matters entirely, for the same ecclesiastics who had rebelled against the signing of the *privilegium* were no more anxious either to pave the way for a Gallican schism or to see the papacy become a tool of French diplomacy. The answer was a council of unquestionable legitimacy, convened by the pope himself, and thus forestalling any such action by the French episcopate. But the attendance at this council was strictly controlled. The letters of convocation were sent out so late as to make any sizable attendance by northern prelates impossible, as a result, only two transalpine bishops were present—Gerard of Angoulême, the eventual proposer of the decree, who arrived late and apparently by chance, and Galo of Paris, a moderate, the testimony of Ordericus Vitalis notwithstanding, as his signature on the letter protesting the council at Anse testifies. In fact, Bruno of Segni was not present at the Lateran, but signed afterwards, and very likely put his name to a decision which he, like so many others, thought to be a condemnation of the emperor.

The council of March 1112 then issued no more than a decision rubber-stamped by its Italian promoters to prevent the immediate problem of French opposition by ostensibly removing the canonical bases for that opposition. The council met explicitly to consider the revocation of the *privilegium* and the status of lay investiture in church doctrine, and thus implicitly was to be the testing-ground for many more basic issues, such as the status of the emperor, the ability of a pope on his own initiative to declare orthodox a practice which former popes, as well as he himself, had declared in council to be heretical, and (in the long run most important of all) whether a pope erring in a matter of faith could be judged and deposed as a heretic. None of these questions, raised in the polemic of the preceding year, were broached at all, but instead a solution was adopted based on a trick of semantics, intended temporarily to satisfy everyone.

Paschal's position in these affairs is unclear. Indeed, it may well be supposed that the pope expected the imminent return of the emperor, a course suggested to Henry by his own Italian correspondents, for the pope was apparently in touch with imperial emissaries soon after the council. At any rate, no sentence of excommunication against Henry was issued by Paschal, and thus by May of 1112 the French king was again applying pressure upon the Gallican clergy to take definite action along the lines of the earlier polemic. On the basis of this interpretation of the Lateran decree the archbishop Guy of Vienne, under the aegis of Louis VI, called a council which met in his city on 16 September. Held under the presidency of Godfrey, bishop of Amiens, at the request of Guy on grounds that a lingual impediment prohibited his chairmanship, the council heard legates from the emperor, who produced letters evidencing the friendly relations between Paschal and Henry even following the council in March. Unable to understand this, the relation of the council informs us, and realizing that the fate of the church was at issue, the council had decided to take the canonical road. The proposal of bishop Hugh of Grenoble, that Henry be excommunicated, was accepted, and the council in three terse sentences condemned lay investiture as a heresy, damned the *privilegium* of April 1111, and anathematized the emperor. Noting that with them stood the people and most of the lay princes, the council called upon the pope to give confirmation to these acts in clear terms, for otherwise the bishops present at Vienne would renounce their obedience to Paschal.

The council at Vienne served to put into effect the principles elaborated by the polemic of the preceding year. Two factors had made such action possible. First was the canonical development which had accompanied the increasing prestige of the papacy in recent years, and which thus made possible the formulation of principles which became the basis for protest against Paschal as having transgressed his power by acting beyond the boundaries of these principles. The second factor was the attainment of a power and interest on the part of the French monarchy sufficient to make the espousal of this protest both possible and desirable. The rapid increase in imperial power was undoubtedly a source of dismay to Louis, as to so many others who could not wish to see the emperor make the papacy once again into his own private property. The answer was a strong opposition, and one that could now find firm arguments to counter the traditional claims of pope and Emperor. The French movement of 1112 could have been the first step in a full-fledged program of Gallicanism; aimed directly at the pope, its intent was either to force his abandonment of the imperial cause or to bring about his deposition (or the secession of the Gallican church) and, we may assume, the election of a new pope, probably Guy of Vienne. Such action was prevented finally by Paschal's confirmation of the decrees of Vienne, and perhaps by Louis' preoccupation with other affairs.

The events of 1111 and 1112 are of vital significance in ecclesiastical history. They find adequate explanation only through the concomitant circumstances of a rapidly developing legal consciousness, a French king ready and able to enhance his position rather than permit his German counterpart to continue toward a possible western hegemony, and a pope unable in the face of various pressures either to adhere firmly to the doctrines of his predecessors or to enunciate a powerful policy of his own. Reaction to the concession of April 1111 not only provided concrete precedent for later Conciliar activity, but nearly anticipated that movement by several hundred years.

After protracted negotiations, the Concordat of Worms (1122) concluded the Investiture Controversy in Germany. It rested on two precedents: separate agreements reached much earlier between the papacy and the kings of France and England. At the end of the conflict, we find as many ambiguities as at the beginning, and this is brought out in the scholarly appraisals.*

Text

The Concordat of Worms (1122)

The *Privilegium* of Henry V

In the name of the holy and indivisible Trinity, I, Henry by the grace of God Emperor Augustus of the Romans, for the love of God and of the holy Roman church and of the Lord Pope Calixtus, and for the cure of my soul, give up to God and to the holy Apostles of God, Peter and Paul, and to the holy catholic Church all investiture by ring and crozier, and I grant that, in all churches which are in my kingdom or empire, there may be canonical election and free consecration.

I restore to the same Roman church such possessions and regalia of St. Peter as I have which were taken away between the beginning of this conflict and the pres-

ent day, whether in the time of my father or in my own; and I shall faithfully assist to the end that those which I do not have may be restored.

With the counsel of princes, and by justice, I shall also give back such possessions as I have of all other churches and princes and others, both clergy and laymen, which were lost in this war, and I shall faithfully assist to the end that those which I do not have be given back.

And I give true peace to the Lord Pope Calixtus and to the Roman church and to all who are, or have been, on its side.

And I shall faithfully assist in such matters as the holy Roman church asks aid, and I shall do the justice due it in such things as it complains about.

---

*From *Monumenta Germaniae Historica, Constitutiones*, vol. 1 (Hannover, 1893), pp. 159ff, 161. Translated by Karl F. Morrison.

All these things have been enacted with the consent and counsel of the princes whose names are subscribed:

Adalbert, Archbishop of Mainz
Frederick, Archbishop of Cologne
Henry, Bishop of Regensburg
Otto, Bishop of Bamberg
Bruno, Bishop of Speyer
Herman of Augsburg
Godebald of Trier
Udalrich of Constance
Erlholf, Abbot of Fulda
Duke Henry
Duke Frederick
Duke Simon
Duke Bertolf
Margrave Theobald
Margrave Engelbert
The Palatine Godfrey
The Count Palatine Otto
Count Berengar

I, Frederick, Archbishop of Cologne and Archchancellor, have certified this.

The *Privilegium* of Calixtus II (the Calixtinum)

I, Calixtus, bishop, servant of the servants of God, grant to you, dear son Henry by the grace of God Emperor Augustus of the Romans, that the elections of bishops and abbots of the German kingdom, which are subject to the kingdom, may take place in your presence, without simony or any sort of violence; and that, if any discord emerges among parties, you may, with the counsel and judgment of the metropolitan and comprovincials, give assent and aid to the sounder party. Let the elect, however, receive the regalia from you by the sceptre and do what he rightly owes to you on their account.

But in other parts of the Empire, let him receive the regalia from you by the sceptre within six months after consecration and do what he rightly owes to you on their account, excepting all things which are known to belong to the Roman church.

According to what befits my office, I shall give you aid in such things as you shall make complaint about and ask aid.

I give true peace to you and to all who are on your side or have been on it in the time of this dispute.

JAMES BRYCE, Viscount Bryce (1838–1922), embodied the classical ideal that the man of action was best qualified to write history. His intellectual brilliance led him from childhood in Glasgow to a scholarship at Trinity College, Oxford (1857), to a fellowship at Oriel College (1862), and finally to a Regius Professorship of Civil Law, at Oxford (1870–1893). *The Holy Roman Empire* (1864), his first published work of distinction, was followed by other works sharply focused on legal and constitutional history. He is credited with having revived, almost single-handed, the study of Roman Law at Oxford, and his book *The American Commonwealth* (1888) is still acknowledged as an authoritative study of the American constitution. While these impressive works were under way, Bryce pursued a glittering career in politics. A member of Parliament (1880–1907), he served the Cabinet in several positions of responsibility. He represented the United Kingdom as ambassador in Washington (1907–1913), and he worked to support the International Court at The Hague and to establish the League of Nations.*

James Bryce

The Papacy Master of the Field

Reformed by the Emperors and their Teutonic nominees, the Papacy had resumed in the middle of the eleventh century the ambitious schemes shadowed forth by Nicholas I, and which the degradation of the last age had only suspended. Under the guidance of her greatest mind, Hildebrand, the archdeacon of Rome, she now advanced to their completion, and proclaimed that war of the ecclesiastical power against the civil power in the person of the Emperor, which became the centre of the subsequent history of both.

While the nature of the struggle cannot be understood without a glance at their previous connection, the vastness of the subject forbids an attempt to draw even its outlines, and restricts our view to those relations of Popedom and Empire which arise directly out of their respective positions as heads spiritual and temporal of the universal Christian state.

The eagerness of Christianity in the age immediately following her recognition as the religion favoured by the state to purchase by submission the support

*From James Bryce, *The Holy Roman Empire* (New York: The Macmillan Company, 1904), pp. 153–166. Reprinted by permission of St. Martin's Press, The Macmillan Company of Canada, and Macmillan & Company, Ltd., London. Footnotes omitted.

of the civil power, has been already re-marked. The change from independence to supremacy was gradual. The tale we smile at, how Constantine, healed of his leprosy, granted the West to bishop Sylvester, and retired to Byzantium that no secular prince might interfere with the jurisdiction or profane the neighbour-hood of Peter's chair, worked great effects through the belief it commanded for many centuries. Nay more, it had a sort of groundwork in fact. Through the removal of the seat of government from the Tiber to the Bosphorus the Pope grew to be the greatest personage in the city, and in the prostration after Alarich's invasion he was seen to be so. Henceforth he alone was a permanent and effective, though still un-acknowledged power, as truly superior to the senate and consuls in the revived municipal republic after the ninth cen-tury as Augustus and Tiberius had been to the faint continuance of their earlier prototypes. Pope Leo the First asserted the universal jurisdiction of his see, and his persevering successors slowly en-thralled Italy, Illyricum, Gaul, Spain, Af-rica, dexterously confounding their un-doubted metropolitan and patriarchal rights with those of oecumenical bishop, in which they were finally merged. By his writings and the fame of his personal sanc-tity, by the conversion of England and the introduction of an impressive ritual, Gregory the Great did more than any other pontiff to advance Rome's ecclesias-tical authority. Yet his tone to Maurice of Constantinople was deferential, to Phocas adulatory; his successors were not con-secrated till confirmed by the Emperor or the Exarch; one of them was dragged in chains to the Bosphorus, and banished thence to Scythia. When the Image-break-ing controversy and the intervention of Pipin weakened and ultimately broke the allegiance of the Popes to the East,

the Franks, as patricians and Emperors, seemed to step into the position which Constantinople had lost. At Charles's coronation says the Saxon poet,

> Et summus eundem
> Praesul adoravit, sicut mos debitus olim
> Principibus fuit antiquis.[1]

Their relations were, however, no longer the same. If the Frank vaunted conquest, the priest spoke only of free gift. What Christendom saw was that Charles was crowned by the Pope's hands, and under-took as his principal duty the protection and advancement of the Holy Roman Church. The circumstances of Otto the Great's coronation gave an even more favourable opening to sacerdotal claims, for it was a Pope who summoned him to Rome and a Pope who received from him an oath of fidelity and aid, as it had been through the action of successive pontiffs that the fleeting Emperors of the preced-ing hundred years had each obtained the crown. In the conflict of three powers, the Emperor, the pontiff, and the people—represented by their senate and consuls, or by the demagogue of the hour—the most steady, prudent, and far-sighted was sure eventually to prevail. The Popedom had no minorities, as yet few disputed successions, few revolts within its own army—the host of churchmen through Europe. The conversion of Germany by the English Winfrith (St. Boniface), under its direct sanction, gave it a hold on the rising hierarchy of the greatest European state; the extension of the rule of Charles and Otto diffused in the same measure its emissaries and pretensions. The first disputes turned on the right of the prince to confirm the elected pontiff, which was afterwards supposed to have been granted

---

[1] [And the Supreme Pontiff [i.e., the Pope] bowed in adoration before him, as once had been the obser-vance due ancient princes.—Ed.]

by Hadrian I to Charles, in the decree quoted as *"Hadrianus Papa."* This *"ius eligendi et ordinandi summum pontificem"* [the right of electing and ordaining the Supreme Pontiff], which Lewis I appears as abandoning by the *"Ego Ludovicus,"* was claimed by the Carolingians whenever they felt themselves strong enough, and having fallen into desuetude in the troublous times of the Italian Emperors, was formally renewed to Otto the Great by his nominee Leo VIII. We have seen it used, and used in the purest spirit, by Otto himself, by his grandson Otto III, last of all, and most autocratically, by Henry III. Along with it there had grown up a bold counter-assumption of the papal chair to be itself the source of the imperial dignity. In submitting to a fresh coronation by the Pope, Lewis the Pious tacitly admitted the invalidity of that previously performed by his father: Charles the Bald did not scout the arrogant declaration of John VIII, that to him alone the Emperor owed his crown; and the council of Pavia, when it chose that monarch king of Italy, repeated the assertion. Subsequent Popes knew better than to apply to the chiefs of Saxon and Franconian chivalry language which the feeble Neustrian had not resented; but the precedent remained, the weapon was only hid behind the pontifical robe to be flashed out with effect when the moment should come. There were also two other great steps which papal power had taken. By the invention or adoption of the False Decretals it had provided itself with a legal system suited to any emergency, and which gave it unlimited authority through the Christian world in causes spiritual and over persons ecclesiastical. Canonistical ingenuity found it easy in one way or another to make this include all causes and persons whatsoever: for crime is always, and wrong is often, sin, nor can aught be anywhere

done which may not affect the clergy. On the gifts of Pipin and Charles, repeated and confirmed by Lewis I, Charles II, Otto I, and Otto III, and now made to rest on the more venerable authority of the first Christian Emperor, it could found claims to the sovereignty of Rome, Tuscany, and all else that had belonged to the exarchate. Indefinite in their terms, these grants were not meant by the donors to convey full political authority over the districts bestowed—that belonged to the head of the Empire—but only, as in the case of other church estates, a sort of perpetual usufruct, a beneficial enjoyment which did not carry sovereignty, but might be deemed to carry a sort of feudal lordship over the tenants who dwelt upon the soil. They were, in fact, what we should call endowments. Nor had the gifts been ever actually reduced into possession: the Pope had been hitherto more frequently the victim than the lord of the neighbouring barons. The grants were, however, not denied, and might be made a formidable engine of attack. Appealing to them, the Pope could brand his opponents as unjust and impious; and could summon nobles and cities to defend him as their liege lord, just as, with no better original right, he subsequently invoked the help of the Norman conquerors of Naples and Sicily.

The attitude of the Roman Church to the imperial power at Henry the Third's death was externally respectful. The title of a German king to receive the crown of the city was not seriously disputed and the Pope was his lawful subject. Hitherto the initiative in reform had come from the civil magistrate. But the secret of the pontiff's strength lay in this: he, and he alone, could confer the crown, and had therefore the right of imposing conditions on its recipient. Frequent interregna, while they had enabled the Pope to assume upon each occasion a more and more independent position, had prevented the power of the Transalpine sovereigns from taking firm root. None of them could claim to reign by hereditary right: none could deny that the holy Church had before sought and might again seek a defender elsewhere. And since the need of such defence had originated the "transference of the Empire from the Greeks to the Franks," since to render such defence was the Emperor's chief function, the Pope might surely hold it to be his duty as well as his right to see that the candidate was capable of fulfilling his task, to reject him if he neglected or misperformed it.

The first step was to remove a blemish in the constitution of the Church, by fixing a defined body to choose the supreme pontiff. This Nicholas II did in A.D. 1059, under the counsel and impulse of the archdeacon Hildebrand. His decree vested the election in the college of cardinals, while it contemplated the subsequent assent of the clergy and people of Rome and reserved the rights of Henry IV and more vaguely of his successors. Then the reforming spirit, kindled by the abuses and depravity of the last century, advanced apace. Directed by Hildebrand, who after having exerted a predominant influence during two pontificates himself became Pope as Gregory the Seventh in A.D. 1073, it strove for two main objects—the enforcement of celibacy, especially on the secular clergy, who enjoyed in this respect considerable freedom; and the extinction of simony. In the former, the Emperors and part of the laity were not unwilling to join: the latter no one dared to defend in theory. But when Gregory declared that it was sin for the ecclesiastic to receive his benefice under conditions from a layman, and so condemned the whole system of the feudal investitures of land to the clergy, he aimed a deadly blow at the authority of every secular ruler. Half of the land and wealth of Germany was in the hands of bishops and abbots, who would now be freed from the Emperor's control to pass under that of the Pope. In such a state of things government itself would be impossible.

Henry and Gregory already mistrusted each other: after this decree war was inevitable. The Pope cited his opponent to appear and be judged at Rome for his vices and misgovernment. The Emperor replied by convoking a synod, which deposed and insulted Gregory. At once the dauntless monk pronounced Henry excommunicate, and fixed a day on which, if still unrepentant, he should cease to reign. Supported by his own princes, the monarch might have defied a command backed by no external force; but the Saxons, never contented since the first place had passed from their own dukes to the Franconians, only waited the signal to burst into a new revolt, whilst through all Germany the Emperor's tyranny and irregularities of life had sown the seeds of disaffection. Shunned, betrayed, threatened, he rushed into what seemed the only course left, and Canossa saw Europe's mightiest prince, titular lord of the world, a suppliant before the successor of the Apostle. Henry soon found that his humiliation had not served him; driven back into opposition, he defied Gregory anew, set up an anti-pope, overthrew the rival whom his rebellious subjects had raised, and maintained to the end of his sad and chequered life a power often depressed but never destroyed. Nevertheless had all other humiliation been spared, that one scene in the yard of the Countess Matilda's castle, an imperial penitent standing barefoot and woollen-frocked on the snow, till the priest who sat within should admit and absolve him, was enough to mark a decisive change, and inflict an irretrievable disgrace on the crown so abased. Its wearer could no more, with the same lofty confidence, claim to be the highest power on earth, created by and answerable to God alone. Gregory had extorted the recognition of that absolute superiority of spiritual authority which he was wont to assert so sternly, proclaiming that to the Pope, as God's Vicar, all mankind are subject, and all rulers responsible, so that he, the giver of the crown, may also excommunicate and depose. And he discovered a simile which played a great part in subsequent controversy, a simile so happily suited to the modes of thought of the Middle Ages that no one dreamt of denying that it expressed the meaning of Scripture and the purpose of the Creator. Writing to William the Conqueror, king of England, he says: "For as for the beauty of this world, that it may be at different seasons perceived by fleshly eyes, God hath disposed the Sun and the Moon, lights that outshine all others; so lest the creature whom His goodness hath formed after His own image in this world should be drawn astray into fatal dangers, He hath provided in the apostolic and royal dignities the means of ruling it through divers offices. . . . If I, therefore, am to answer for thee on the dreadful day of judgment before the just Judge who cannot lie, the creator of every creature, bethink thee whether I must not very diligently provide for thy salvation, and whether, for thine own safety, thou oughtest not without delay to obey me, that so thou mayest possess the land of the living."

Gregory was not the inventor or first propounder of these doctrines; they had been before his day a part of mediaeval Christianity, interwoven with its most vital doctrines. Six centuries earlier Pope Gelasius I had implicitly stated them in a letter enjoining obedience on the Em-

peror Anastasius. They were held by many others in Gregory's day, and expressed with a more militant vehemence by his contemporary and friend Alfanus of Salerno. But Gregory was the first who dared to apply them to the world as he found it. His was the rarest and grandest of gifts, an intellectual courage and power of imaginative belief which, when it has convinced itself of aught, accepts it fully with all its consequences, and shrinks not from acting at once upon it. A perilous gift, as the melancholy end of his own career proved, for men were found less ready than he had thought them to follow out with unswerving consistency like his the principles which all acknowledged. But it was the very suddenness and boldness of his policy that secured the ultimate triumph of his cause, awing men's minds and making that seem realized which had been till then a vague theory. His premises once admitted—and no one dreamt of denying them—the reasonings by which he established the superiority of spiritual to temporal jurisdiction were unassailable. With his authority, in whose hands are the keys of heaven and hell, whose word can bestow eternal bliss or plunge in everlasting misery, no earthly potentate can compete or interfere. If his power extends into the infinite, how much more must he be supreme over things finite? It was thus that Gregory and his successors were wont to argue: the wonder is, not that they were obeyed, but that they were not obeyed more implicitly. In the second sentence of excommunication which Gregory passed upon Henry the Fourth are these words:

"Come now, I beseech you, O most holy and blessed Fathers and Princes, Peter and Paul, that all the world may understand and know that if ye are able to bind and to loose in heaven, ye are likewise able on earth, according to the merits of each man, to give and to take away empires, kingdoms, princedoms, marquisates, duchies, countships, and the possessions of all men. For if ye judge spiritual things, what must we believe to be your power over worldly things? and if ye judge the angels who rule over all proud princes, what can ye not do to their slaves?"

Doctrines such as these do indeed strike equally at all temporal governments, nor were the Innocents and Bonifaces of later days slow to apply them so. On the Empire, however, the blow fell first and heaviest. As when Alarich entered Rome, the spell of ages was broken, Christendom saw its stateliest and most venerable institution dishonoured and helpless; allegiance was no longer undivided, for who could presume to fix in each case the limits of the civil and ecclesiastical jurisdictions? The potentates of Europe beheld in the Papacy a force which, if dangerous to themselves, could be made to repel the pretensions and baffle the designs of the strongest and haughtiest among them. Italy learned how to meet the Teutonic conqueror by gaining papal sanction for the leagues of her cities. The German princes, anxious to narrow the prerogative of their head, were the natural allies of his enemy, whose spiritual thunders, more terrible than their own lances, could enable them to depose an aspiring monarch, or extort from him any concessions they desired. Their altered tone is marked by the promise they required from Rudolf of Swabia, whom, at the Pope's suggestion, they set up as a rival to Henry, that he would not endeavor to make the throne hereditary.

It is not possible here to dwell on the details of the great struggle of the Investitures, rich as it is in the interest of adventure and character, momentous as were its results for the future. A word or two must suffice to describe the conclusion, not indeed of the whole drama, which was to extend over centuries, but of what may be called its first act. Even that act lasted beyond the lives of the original performers. Gregory the Seventh passed away at Salerno in A.D. 1085, exclaiming with his last breath, "I have loved justice and hated iniquity, therefore I die in exile." Twenty-one years later Henry IV died, dethroned by an unnatural son whom the hatred of a relentless pontiff had raised in rebellion against him. But that son, the Emperor Henry the Fifth, so far from conceding the points in dispute, proved an antagonist more ruthless and not less able than his father. He claimed for his crown all the rights over ecclesiastics that his predecessors had ever enjoyed, and when at his coronation in Rome, A.D. 1111, Pope Paschal II refused to complete the rite until he should have yielded, Henry seized both Pope and cardinals and compelled them by a rigorous imprisonment to consent to a treaty which he dictated. Once set free, the Pope, as was natural, disavowed his extorted concessions, and the struggle was protracted for ten years longer, until nearly half a century had elapsed from the first quarrel between Gregory VII and Henry IV. The Concordat of Worms, concluded between Pope Calixtus II and Henry V, provided for the freedom of ecclesiastical elections and the renunciation by the Emperor of investiture by the ring and the crozier, but it left to him the right of investing the clergy with all temporalities by the sceptre, and the right to require from them (except those who held directly from the Pope) the performance of their duties as feudal vassals. This settlement was in form a compromise, designed to spare either party the humiliation of defeat. Yet the Papacy remained master of the field. The Emperor retained but one-half of those rights of investiture which had formerly been his. He could never resume the position of Henry III; his wishes or intrigues might influence the proceedings of a chapter, his oath bound him from open interference. He had entered the strife in the fullness of dignity; he came out of it with tarnished glory and shattered power. His wars had been hitherto carried on with foreign foes, or at worst with a single rebel noble; now his former ally was turned into his fiercest assailant, and had enlisted against him half his court, half the magnates of his realm. At any moment his sceptre might be shivered in his hand by the bolt of anathema, and a host of enemies spring up from every convent and cathedral.

Two other results of this great conflict ought not to pass unnoticed. The Emperor was alienated from the Church at the most unfortunate of all moments, the era of the Crusades. To conduct a great religious war against the enemies of the faith, to head the church militant in her carnal as the Popes were accustomed to do in her spiritual strife, this was the very purpose for which an Emperor had been called into being; and it was indeed in these wars, more particularly in the first three of them, that the ideal of a Christian commonwealth, embodied in the theory of the mediaeval Empire, was once for all and never again realized by the combined action of the great nations of Europe. Had such an opportunity fallen to the lot of Henry III, he might have used it to win back a supremacy such as had belonged to the first Carolingians. But Henry IV's proscription excluded him from all share in an enterprise which he must otherwise have led—nay more, committed it to the guidance of his foes. The religious feeling which the crusades evoked—a feeling which became the origin of the great orders of chivalry, and somewhat later of the two great orders of mendicant friars—turned against the power which resisted ecclesiastical claims, and was made to work the will of the Holy See, which had blessed and organized the project. A century and a half later the Pope did not scruple to preach a crusade against the Emperor himself.

Again, it was now that the first seeds were sown of that fear and hatred wherewith many among the German people never thenceforth ceased to regard the encroaching Romish court. Branded by the Church and forsaken by the nobles, Henry IV retained the affections of the burghers of Worms and Liége. It soon became the test of Teutonic patriotism to resist Italian priestcraft.

The changes in the internal constitution of Germany due to the long anarchy of Henry IV's reign are seen when the extent of the royal prerogative as it had stood at the accession of Conrad II, the first Franconian Emperor, is compared with its state at Henry V's death. All fiefs are now hereditary, and when vacant can be granted afresh only by consent of the States; the jurisdiction of the crown is less wide; the idea is beginning to make progress that the most essential part of the Empire is not its supreme head but the totality of princes and barons. The greatest triumph of these feudal magnates is seen in the establishment of the elective principle, which when confirmed by the three free elections of Lothar II, Conrad III, and Frederick I, passes into an undoubted law. The Prince-Electors are mentioned in A.D. 1156 as a distinct and important body. The bishops, too, whom the policy of Otto the Great and Henry II had raised, are now not less dangerous than the dukes, whose power it was hoped they would balance; possibly more dangerous, since protected by their sacred character and their allegiance to the Pope, while able at the same time to command the arms of their countless vassals. Nor were the two succeeding Emperors the men to retrieve those disasters. The Saxon Lothar the Second is the willing minion of the Pope; performs at his coronation a menial service unknown before, and takes a more stringent oath to defend the Holy See, that he may purchase its support against the Swabian party in his own dominions. Conrad the Third, the first Emperor of the great house of Hohenstaufen, represents tendencies more anti-papal; but domestic toubles and an unfortunate crusade prevented him from effecting anything in Italy. He never even entered Rome to receive the crown.

The Right Reverend JOHN TRACY ELLIS (b.1905) is
an eminent educator and writer on Church history.
For more than twenty years (1941–1963) he served as
managing editor of the *Catholic Historical Review.* In
1964, he became professor of church history at the
University of San Francisco. *Anti-papal Legislation
in Medieval England* (1930) was his first book. More
recent works have dealt with major currents in
American intellectual life.*

John Tracy Ellis

The Agreement of London:
A Distinct Victory for the Lay Power

In considering the relations of William
the Conqueror with the papacy, it is necessary for us to look to the continent in
order to learn what was transpiring in
Europe immediately preceding and during the Conqueror's English reign. The
latter half of the eleventh century saw a
determined effort on the part of the popes
to rid the administration of Church affairs of the interference of secular princes.
Pope Leo IX (1049–1054) was the first of
the sovereign pontiffs of this period to
show clearly how the pope might aspire
to rule emperors and kings, and actually
make the papacy the overlord of Europe.
Shortly after his accession to the papal
throne Leo demonstrated his resoluteness
of purpose in this regard by enacting,
through a decree of the Synod of Rheims,
that for the future no candidate for the
office of bishop should receive episcopal
consecration who had not been elected
first by the clergy and people. He made
it very plain that he felt entirely independent of Emperor Henry III (1039–1056),
the man who had been most instrumental
in placing him in his present high position. Pope Nicholas II (1058–1061) in
April, 1059 took the election of the popes
out of the hands of the German emperors
and secular authorities, and instituted
the college of cardinals for that purpose,
which left the emperor and the other
princes with very little immediate influence in the filling of that office. The reason for this act of Nicholas II can be found

*From John Tracy Ellis, *Anti-Papal Legislation in Medieval England (1066-1377)* (Washington, D.C.:
The Catholic University of America Press, 1930), pp. 6–23. Footnotes omitted.

in the frightful confusion which frequently attended a papal election in which the emperor and the rival factions of the Roman nobility had a voice. The example of the shameful election of the anti-pope, Benedict X, in April, 1058, which was brought about by the nobility of Rome and which resulted in trouble and misfortune for all, was fresh in the mind of Pope Nicholas.

However, the efforts to free the government of the Church from secular influence made by these popes was not to go unchallenged. Upon the accession of Pope Gregory VII (1073–1085), with his exalted ideals of reform and his determination to cleanse the Church of her political and simoniacal abuses and corruption, we see the beginning of that long conflict between the popes and the emperors which was to culminate in the complete subjection of the latter, but only after a struggle which stretched over almost two hundred years, and which left both parties well nigh exhausted.

Gregory's great adversary was the Emperor Henry IV (1065–1106). It is unnecessary for us to enter into the details of the conflict. It arose over the determination of Gregory, issued in a strong prohibition in 1075, to end lay investitures. The action of Gregory in sending legates to Henry, the highhanded response of the emperor, who was angered by the language which the legates employed, his excommunication and deposition, his submission at Canossa in 1077, his second excommunication and final triumph over the aged Gregory, when he was joined by his German nobles and clergy following the second excommunication—all these are well known facts to the student of history. The point to be made in connection with this study is the part being played by the Conqueror in England during these eventful years.

From the very outset William's relations with the Holy See were cordial. He had appealed to Rome for approval of his invasion of England, promising Pope Alexander II that if he received the papal sanction to his venture, he would bring the English Church and clergy into closer submission to the Roman See. Therefore Alexander, being moved by this promise of William, as also by the wish expressed by Edward the Confessor (1043–1066) before his death that William should succeed him, encouraged William in his expedition and blessed his cause. . . . William had early sent for the pope's legates to help him reform the administration of the English Church and the pope had graciously consented. Alexander gave outward expression to the spirit of good will which characterized the negotiations between the two rulers in a letter which he wrote to the Conqueror, praising him for his great faith and the devotion he had manifested in the cause of religion in England, as well as the support he had given to the efforts of Lanfranc.

However, William was not long established in England before he made it very clear that he was to be the complete master of the new kingdom. In a letter to Pope Gregory, sent some time during the year 1076–1077, the exact date of which is doubtful, the Conqueror expressed his refusal to do homage to Gregory or his successors for the kingdom of England because, as he said, he had never promised it and his predecessors had never done homage to Gregory's predecessors. The pope, so it would seem, since we have no document containing Gregory's request, had made his demand on the strength of the superiority of the spiritual over the temporal power. As the spiritual overlord of all feudal dependencies the pope claimed fealty, since he was to represent these dependencies before the judgment seat of God. In this instance the pope was not making demands upon England alone, for we find him receiving an oath of fealty and homage from Robert of Normandy in June, 1080 for the lands which that prince held of the papacy. He also made similar claims to Spain, Corsica, and Sardinia on the basis of the Donation of Constantine, and to Hungary because of King Stephen's act of homage to the papacy for his kingdom. William therefore by his refusal to do homage to Hildebrand was creating a precedent for independent action upon the part of future English kings. We shall see that this precedent was not the only one set by William in shaping the English policy toward Rome.

Besides laying down this declaration of independent action from Rome, the Conqueror had no small share in putting into operation the machinery by which that declaration might be rendered effective. He made it understood that he would not allow any pope to be recognized in England without his consent; no papal bulls or letters were to enter the country without the royal permission; no council was to enact a canon or forbid anything, or no bishop or ecclesiastic was to excommunicate any of his barons without having first ascertained the Conqueror's pleasure in the matter. These and many other minor details William reserved entirely to himself. Gregory complained of these bold assertions of William, but he did not take action against them. He even allowed William to select ecclesiastics of his own choice to fill the high church offices in England. Gregory therefore did not challenge the Conqueror on any of the assumed powers of that ruler, a fact which will bear further explanation.

The reason for this leniency is undoubtedly to be found in this fact. Pope Greg-

ory was engaged in possibly the greatest struggle in the history of the papacy up to that time with the emperor over the question of investitures. He needed the good will and support of the English king, and therefore it would have been pure folly for him to insist upon William obeying these various strictures. Moreover William and Archbishop Lanfranc were not slow to realize their advantage. When the anti-pope, Clement, was elected in 1080 at Brixen it gave Lanfranc and the Conqueror a weapon with which to threaten Gregory, should the pontiff push his claims too far in England. Lanfranc did not recognize Clement, though he inferred that he might do so, which held Gregory in check for fear of losing England's support. His position was extremely dangerous, for at this time the Emperor Henry was marching upon Rome. Lanfranc proved the diplomat by withholding his support from Clement, but at the same time hinting at the possibility of recognition. The archbishop was in this instance more the diplomat than the loyal son of the Holy See, for he was in sympathy with the Conqueror, who was anxious lest the papacy secure too much liberty in the direction of the affairs of the English Church.

Confronted by this opposition from William and Lanfranc and imperiled by the force of the imperial power, Gregory was not able to press his demands upon the English monarch. And although this question of the investitures, the receiving of papal bulls and legates certainly did play an important part in the life of the Church, Rome was able nevertheless to draw the fine distinction between these questions and matters which would touch her spiritual existence, the heritage of which she must guard uncompromisingly. William was strong, the papacy was trembling in the balance for its life as a power in the affairs of Europe, hence there was but one thing to do and that was to temporize.

This she did. But the dangerous precedent set by this great liberty and freedom given to the Conqueror in England was to have its effect in the years to come. The Conqueror's successors, especially his two sons, looked back with longing glances at the unrestrained freedom allowed him in the affairs of the Church, and it was not so many years before they were claiming this prerogative of freedom, sometimes to their sorrow. William I was a conscientious ruler and a devout son of the faith, who possessed a deep reverence for the sovereign pontiff. A number of his successors regarded the faith but lightly and considered the papacy only as an object for their greed. The Holy See was to suffer at their hands for the dangerous leniency with which it treated the Conqueror.

Aside from quelling the revolt in Normandy begun by Robert, William's son, in 1078, aided as he was by many Norman barons, the defeat of Robert at Gerberci in 1079, and the enforcing of the feudal principles upon his half-brother, Bishop Odo, the earl of Kent, in 1082, there is little to record in the remaining years of the Conqueror's reign, but the great survey of the kingdom which he ordered and which resulted in the Domesday Book. This survey was commanded by William at Christmas, 1085 in order that he might ascertain the financial and military strength of his realm. The goods of the clerical barons were subjected to the scrutiny of the survey as well as those of the lay lords.

In September of 1087 the Conqueror was on the continent pursuing a war against the French king for the possession of the Vexin, a small province lying on the borderland between France and Nor-

mandy. While here he met with an accident which resulted in his death. On his deathbed he dictated his choice of successor as William, his favorite son.

The effects of the conquest of England by the Normans were far-reaching, and were not to manifest themselves entirely for many years to come. In the sphere of foreign relations it increased intercourse between the continent and England in trade, diplomacy, and travel. English soldiers engaged in warfare upon the continent, and English ecclesiastics were called to fill positions in continental churches and schools. In government it greatly strengthened the royal power by retention of the old English privileges and the addition of feudal rights, though the changes made were not essentially new and the Conqueror retained the Anglo-Saxon laws and institutions. The king could now command national resources as king, and military service of his vassals as feudal lord. Feudal ideas also reacted on the crown, which became a right of inheritance and not of election. In language we see a gradual loss of English inflexions and a large addition of French words. The English and French exist side by side for a long time, the former the language of the people, the latter of the court. When English again came into general use it had undergone a profound transformation due to this fusion with the French.

But it is in the affairs of the Church that we are most interested. The Conquest witnessed the increase of papal influence within the Church itself under Hildebrand. Likewise a closer union of Church and state in England became evident with the liberty and freedom granted to the Conqueror in administering the appointments to benefices, etc. The establishment of the ecclesiastical courts and their separation from the legislative assemblies by William contributed to the power of the papacy in England and produced a great effect upon later legislation. Lastly there was the great reform in the discipline of the clergy which came into England following the Conquest, and which William encouraged in order to bring the English Church into closer harmony with the churches on the continent which had felt the effects of the reform movement.

The England left by the Conqueror upon his death to his son and successor, William II (1087–1100), was a kingdom much more unified and compact than he had found it in 1066. Aside from a revolt in 1088 led by Odo, the king's uncle, who rose in support of Robert of Normandy, the signing of the Treaty of Caen in 1091, by which William II and Robert agreed that whoever should die first his successor should inherit both kingdoms, the pledging of Normandy by Robert to William when he was about to start on the crusade in 1096, and another desultory war with France in 1098 over the possession of Le Maine, little of political interest took place during this reign. The chief feature of these years was the struggle between William and Anselm, the archbishop of Canterbury.

By the year 1089, the year of Lanfranc's death, the effects of the great Gregorian Reform had begun to exercise a permanent benefit in England. The introduction of the continentals from France and Normandy had brought into England the spirit of the movement which had taken such firm root in Europe, and it was inevitable that the results of that movement, which had so nearly changed the face of a continent before it came to an end, should now manifest its influence in Britain. Clerical celibacy began to be enforced, episcopal sees were moved from small villages to great centers of population,

the life of the monasteries was made more regular, and schools were opened in large numbers. The whole moral temper of the lower clergy was likewise elevated.

There was at the court of William II a counselor of the king, Ranulf Flambard, a man wholly perverted by a greed for money and dead to the effects of the reform. It was at the promptings of this person that William left the see of Canterbury vacant for four years following the death of Lanfranc. The death of Archbishop Lanfranc had removed the saving restraint placed upon the actions of the king. At last in 1093 William being struck with a strange disease, the nature of which caused the king to fear for his recovery, he consented to have the see filled. The man chosen to head the English hierarchy was Anselm (1093–1109), abbot of Bec. Anselm was born about 1033 and had been connected with the abbey of Bec since 1060, having been its abbot since 1078. As abbot he had occasion to visit England a number of times. During these visits he had won the esteem and respect of all who met him. He was not only a highly spiritual man, but also one of the greatest of medieval Christian philosophers. Anselm enjoyed a wide reputation for scholarship and learning. It was at a time when Anselm happened to be in England on business for his monastery that the king was persuaded to name him archbishop of Canterbury. It was only after a struggle, however, that the abbot could be prevailed upon to accept the grave responsibilities of this office. It was not at all to his liking. It may be that Anselm foresaw the difficulties which it involved. But there seemed to be no other man quite so suited to fulfill the duties of the archbishopric. There was very little doubt but that this appointment would result in conflict, for the king and the archbishop-elect differed widely in their interpretations of Church government, discipline, and reform.

After seven months of hesitation Anselm at length was invested with all the marks of his office by William, and received the archepiscopal consecration in December, 1093. Already the liberty granted to the Conqueror was beginning to bear fruit. His son, a far lesser man, had kept the see vacant four years because he claimed he enjoyed the same right as had been given to his father to fill the episcopal sees at his discretion. He invested the new archbishop with the ring and the staff, the emblems of his spiritual jurisdiction, because his father had been allowed to do likewise. We shall see how the Church was compelled to pursue a very different policy toward this monarch in order to preserve the dignity of her position in England.

The fundamental differences in character between the archbishop and the king soon brought them into conflict. Trouble arose between them over the wish of Anselm to go to Rome for the *pallium,* as was the custom of the time. The king at first refused permission for this journey, claiming that he had not yet recognized Pope Urban II (1088–1099) himself, and hence would not allow one of his subjects to do so without his consent. He complained too at the customary gift offered to him by Anselm upon the latter's promotion. Anselm had presented the king with five hundred pounds which William refused as unworthy of the royal acceptance. William also threatened to recognize the anti-pope, Clement, the puppet of the German emperor, knowing, however, that Clement had no lawful right to the papacy. Again he was putting into practice a privilege reserved by his father, that of allowing a pope to be recognized in England only with his consent. But Anselm met every attack with vigor and

defended with heroic courage the principle that the Universal Church could not suffer the restrictions of a particular ruler in a particular province. The archbishop also stood out against William refusing to recognize papal legates in England without his assent having been given to their mission, and his forbidding Church councils to be held without his approval.

Meanwhile William saw that his methods of coercion were not netting him any advantage in his controversy with the archbishop, and therefore thinking to outwit Anselm he sent messengers to Rome offering a bargain. William would recognize Urban if Urban would depose Anselm. The pope agreed to send a legate to adjust the difficulties, but when the legate arrived in England he went directly to the king, obtained recognition of Urban throughout the realm, and then refused to depose the archbishop. It was a clever move on the part of the papacy. The Holy See had brought William's envoys to Rome, asking for help—something the Conqueror would not have done—and then acquiescing to their request it had settled the difficulty in its own favor but refused to do the king's bidding and remove Anselm. Rome had won in the first stage of that long struggle between the Church and the English kings. The papacy was rising in power; so was England but not quite so rapidly.

Departing a moment from the struggle we have been witnessing, it would be well to take cognizance of a typical act on the part of William, which illustrates the hardships and abuses with which Anselm had to contend. In 1095 we find the king applying feudal principles to the Church, taking back into his hands the property of that institution upon the death of a bishop so that he might benefit by its revenues. The danger of such measures to the ultimate peace and prosperity of the Church may well be appreciated when we consider the great holdings of the ecclesiastical order, and the peril which would threaten the possessions of the Church if this principle were universally applied. It is an example of the greed practiced by this king in all his dealings with the Church. The possessions of the Church offered William an opportunity to enrich his coffers, a chance which he did not neglect.

The act of the king mentioned above is an instance of a particular piece of legislation which applied to the diocese of Worcester, but we shall find a decree issued by William II, the date of which is not known exactly, but which was issued around 1097, the content of which was far more general and embracing in its restrictions. It reiterated the stand taken by the Conqueror, that no one be allowed to acknowledge the pope without his bidding, or receive a letter from him until the king himself had seen it. This decree likewise forbade the primate, the archbishop of Canterbury, from presiding in councils to ordain or forbid anything save that which had been ordained by the king or was agreeable to him. Furthermore it forbade any bishop to sue publicly or excommunicate or constrain by penalty of ecclesiastical rigor, any of the king's barons or ministers accused of capital crimes, without the monarch's permission. This act merely assumed the stand taken by the Conqueror when he made it evident to the pope that he was the sole master of England. Again precedent was playing an important role in the relations between England and Rome.

In the face of such abuses and boldness on the part of the king, his own personal vices, and the corruption of the secular clergy, Anselm was led to appeal in 1097 for permission to go to Rome and plead for papal action against the degeneration of religious discipline and Church government in England. As might be expected William refused the request, ignoring the letters of Anselm. However, the great archbishop was not daunted, making a second and third request, and finally informing William that he would act with or without his permission. At last William gave way before the courage and strength of the primate, realizing no doubt that he could not hope to swerve the archbishop from his sense of duty. William and Anselm parted company in the middle of October, 1097 never to meet again.

Anselm proceeded to Rome and later played an important part in the proceedings of the Council of Bari. William seized the goods and revenues of Canterbury in the occupant's absence, and made off for Normandy to wage another war upon France for the Vexin. Very little of interest transpires in the intervening period between Anselm's departure and the king's death. In August, 1100, King William suffered an accident while hunting, the effect of which brought the monarch to an untimely death. It was left for Henry I (1100–1135), his younger brother, to continue the quarrel with Anselm.

Henry I came to rule England in August, 1100. He was a young, gallant, intelligent, and industrious prince with promising capacities for kingship. All seemed in his favor. One of the first moves of the new king was the imprisonment of Flambard, the sycophant whom his brother had made the justiciar and bishop of Durham. He then recalled Anselm. He had sent a very friendly letter to the archbishop, explaining why it was necessary for him to be crowned before Anselm reached England on account of internal disorders, promising all friendliness, money to convey him home, and every possible consideration. This letter reveals the fact that Henry was anxious to show the archbishop and the pope that he was well disposed toward a peaceable settlement of their differences.

The issuance of his Charter of Liberties in the week following his coronation seemed to substantiate the sincerity of Henry, for in that document—the first written record of feudal monarchy in England, its limits and its dues—Henry promised to make the Church free, neither to sell nor place at rent, nor, when any ecclesiastic should die, to take anything from the domain of the Church or from its men until a successor had been installed. All these pretty promises met their test, however, when Anselm confronted Henry shortly after Michaelmas, 1101 at Salisbury. Again the great issue arose—investitures. Henry asked Anselm to accept the archbishopric from him and to do homage for it. The king was anxious lest the privilege of investiture of bishops, enjoyed by his father and brother, should slip from his hands and thereby weaken his control over the English Church. The archbishop refused the request of the king, for during his exile on the continent his ideas on the disputed question had been crystallized by attendance at the councils where the principle of canonical elections to Church offices by churchmen had been firmly stated and reaffirmed.

We must endeavor to see the principles involved in this conflict in the light of both parties. Though Europe had witnessed in Henry's lifetime the gigantic struggle between the papacy and the empire over this question of investitures, Henry was not without precedent for his determined stand in England. The process of lay investiture had taken deep root in the Church life of Britain during almost two hundred years preceding Henry's reign. It was part of the Anglo-Saxon practice of filling Church offices. It had thus far gone practically unmolested. As we have noted the zeal of Pope Gregory was stirred to uproot this interference with Church government. But despite this zeal Gregory had granted special exceptions to William the Conqueror. His successors, William II and Henry I, sensed the value of these exceptions. On the other hand the Universal Church had now risen to put down this abuse and to restore the government of its offices into its own hands. Anselm was the personification of this spirit of reform in England. Churchmen such as the archbishop felt that the civil authority's interference with the composition of the hierarchy could only make for an ultimate loss of the faith and the mismanagement of Church affairs. It was then an extremely vexacious problem, fraught with many difficulties and bound by traditions of long standing on both sides.

Therefore we find the tradition of years behind Henry, and particularly the recent papal toleration of freedom in Church matters shown towards his father. What feudal king would feel obligated to relinquish this power tolerated in his predecessor not forty years before? The king needed revenue, and if the clergy were suddenly freed from secular bonds bankruptcy of the realm might result, for the clerical party owned a large share of the kingdom's lands. The same was true of the recruiting of military power, for the great bishops and abbots furnished many soldiers for the army of the king. Hence we see Henry caught between the all-embracing sweep of the restoration of the Church's freedom, which was carrying all Europe with it, and the peculiar situation of his own kingdom, which required the financial and military aid of its ecclesiastical barons in order to preserve its life. Henry decided to beg for time, and called a truce of nine months until the spring of 1101.

Meanwhile the king had to meet an invasion of England by his brother, Robert, who came to claim it in virtue of the Treaty of Caen in 1091. The invasion came to naught, however, for with the assistance of the native English Henry was able to force Robert out of the country, and five years later, in 1106, to defeat and capture him at Tinchebrai and to conquer Normandy.

As regards the internal affairs of the English Church we find Anselm in the Council of Westminster in 1102, enforcing in the canons of that council many of the reforms which had by this time gained firm root on the continent. Among them were the condemnation of simony, insistence upon celibacy amongst the clergy, restrictions upon the bishops in judging secular pleas, the methods to be observed in the conduct and dress of clerics, restrictions upon the monks which prevented them from creating knights, abbots' conduct with regard to their subjects, commanding them to eat with their religious and to occupy the same type of sleeping quarters. In spite of the opposition coming from Henry and his court, the general reform of the Church was now touching all classes of the clerical life and working wholesome benefits.

To return to the question of investitures. The quarrel ran on intermittently for almost seven years after Anselm's return to England in September, 1100. The archbishop remained firm, hoping to save as much as possible of the Gregorian ideal, and Henry, while not anxious to shatter that ideal, was solicitous for his domestic government and the security of his kingdom. Despite the fact that this reform was a laudable undertaking and proposed to bring the Christian Church back to a place of superiority, it must be

admitted that it was indeed only an ideal. It could not possibly be realized in a complete fashion while the bishops and other clerical lords insisted upon holding their vast possessions and serving as the king's nobles. That is the point about which the whole problem turns. What was the king to do for financial and military assistance and the security of unified government if the clerics, who held so much property, were to be suddenly freed from all feudal obligations, as the ideal of Hildebrand, carried to its logical conclusion, would certainly bring about? On the other hand how was the Church to affect any kind of permanent reform in her administrative government and defend her clerical offices against the encroachments of the royal authority, if the right of appointments was not returned to her jurisdiction? Common sense would dictate that either plan was untenable in the society of that day. A compromise was imperative. Each side must relinquish a bit of its original stand or lose all. Henry was not reluctant to go part way, and the pope, still anxious to retain Henry as an ally, was also prone to compromise.

At the suggestion of Henry the elderly archbishop made a trip to Rome in 1103, to try to come to some agreement on the delicate question between pope and king. Henry demonstrated his ungracious temperament by seizing the archbishop's temporalities into his own hands in the absence of the primate from England. It must be kept in mind that the major conflict between the pope and the German emperor was still raging at this time, and the pope needed the good offices of the English monarch to aid him in that menace. After a long period of negotiations, which were carried on between the contending parties, and a threat of excommunication levelled at Henry, Anselm and the king came finally to an agreement at Bec where the famous compromise was settled on August 15th, 1107. The ecclesiastic was to receive the ring and the staff, the emblems of his spiritual authority, from the hands of a representative of the Church, but the temporalities and the right to rule over them, were to be received from the hands of the king like any other baron.

It was a distinct victory for the lay power. That authority stood almost exactly where it did before the controversy opened, free to nominate in practice to vacant sees, and receiving the territorial revenues of the Church under the same feudal conditions. The king had gained his point. Regarding the principle which the Church held intact, namely that of ecclesiastical appointments being bestowed by a representative of the Church, that the king had consented to forego. But in those clauses of the agreement which embraced the paying of feudal dues and taxes to the realm, in which both sides were striving to obtain an advantage, the king gained a decided victory. It was upon a similar basis that the agreement with the emperor came to be settled in 1122 at Worms. The Church retained her principle unimpaired.

Here we see concluded one of the important crises between the papacy and the secular arm. The Church, constantly increasing her supreme control over ecclesiastical matters, a movement which was spreading over Europe since the days of Gregory VII, and anxious to clear herself once and for all of the meddling processes of kings, suffered a severe setback. It was destined that the Church should become the most powerful institution in Europe, embracing all nations, and wielding tremendous influence for good, but the point at which the Gregorian Reform aimed — a complete breaking of the fetters and bonds of kings, which

tended to restrain her absolute power, was not to be attained.

Anselm died three years later during Holy Week of 1109, after having fought a courageous fight and having won for the English Church, if not absolute freedom, at least a much-needed disciplinary reform. The year before he died, in the canons issued from the Council of London in 1108, he forbade the clergy to marry or harbor women, and exacted grave punishments of those who might disobey — excommunication, forfeiture of rights, property, etc. After Anselm's death Henry engaged in a successful war with France and Anjou between 1110 and 1119, and occupied his time crushing revolts in Wales and Normandy.

The only other important feature of this reign of thirty-five years to be noticed, is something which has no direct bearing upon England but which is included within our subject, namely the Concordat of Worms or *Pactum Calixtinum*, signed between Pope Calixtus II (1119–1124) and Emperor Henry V (1106–1125) on September 23rd, 1122. This Concordat settled the mooted and troublesome question of investitures between the empire and the papacy, along the same lines as the compromise of 1107 between the pope and the English king.

It is also significant to point out that after Anselm's death the see of Canterbury was vacant five years, a situation of which the Church could not possibly have approved, but which the power of Henry made possible. In November, 1120 Henry lost his son and heir, William, who was drowned in the wreck of the White Ship. Numerous claimants arose and violent civil conflicts ensued during the last years of Henry's rule, so that when that king breathed his last in the winter of 1135 conditions did not augur well for England's future.

ROBERT L. BENSON (b. 1925), professor of history at
Wesleyan University, is a specialist in the history of
canon law. He stands in a long tradition of German
scholarship which places great emphasis on political
symbolism and philosophy and on the philological
analysis of texts. The excerpt here reproduced from his
book on the office of bishop-elect—that is, a man
elected, but not yet consecrated, as bishop—shows this
cast of thought as applied not only to published sources
but also to manuscript evidence, which Benson studied
in Munich and in Rome.*

Robert L. Benson

The Concordat of Worms:

A Limited Victory for the Emperor

In September of 1122, after a half century of struggle between empire and papacy, the emperor Henry V and the legates
of pope Calixtus II came to an agreement
at Worms. Each side issued a charter em-
bodying its concessions and assurances to
the other party. In many ways, this Concordat of Worms was an unusual treaty,
but in no way was it more extraordinary
than in the number of details which it did
not settle. During the conferences leading
to the Concordat, both sides studied the
documents from earlier papal-imperial
diplomacy, especially the detailed documents from the dramatic negotiations of
1111. Since both parties in 1122 were
aware of the crucial precedents, the sim-

ple brevity of the Concordat's two charters was deliberate. In general, the Concordat had both the virtues and the de-
fects of an armistice, for like any truce, its
main purpose was to halt the fighting, and
it provided no fundamental remedy for
the causes of the conflict. Intended as a
practical compromise, the Concordat attempted neither a doctrinaire separation
of Church and monarchy—the fiasco of
February 1111 was sufficient warning—
nor the complete fulfillment of either
party's objectives.

In the imperial charter, Henry V renounced "investiture with ring and crosier," and he promised "canonical election
and free consecration" for the bishops and

---

*From Robert L. Benson, *The Bishop-Elect. A Study in Medieval Ecclesiastical Office* (Princeton, N.J.:
Princeton University Press, 1968), pp. 228–234, 237–239, 242, 247–263. Reprinted by permission of Princeton University Press. Footnotes omitted.

abbots of his empire. With the guarantee of "canonical election," Henry abandoned the long-standing imperial practice of directly appointing bishops. The emperor made these concessions explicitly to the Roman Church, which never dies, and consequently the concessions were permanently binding on his successors. Since Henry's renunciation of the traditional right of investiture was a revolutionary act, a formal grant in perpetuity was legally indispensable.

Through its personal style of address, however, Calixtus II's privilege had formal validity for Henry V, but not for his successors on the imperial throne. This stylistic usage did not necessarily imply that the various rights conceded by Calixtus would disappear with Henry V's death. Rather, Henry and the German princes undoubtedly considered these concessions an already well-grounded part of imperial custom. From this standpoint, the Calixtinum was more a recognition (or, one might almost say, a confirmation) of certain existing rights than a grant of new ones. Indeed, a personal charter valid during Henry's lifetime may have seemed the appropriate form, since it would discourage the inference that traditional imperial rights were based upon papal generosity. Certainly, however, the papal Curia was anxious to assert the personal character of the Calixtinum, and most probably, Henry and the princes would have preferred the obvious future advantages of a perpetual grant, but were unable to win this concession in the hard bargaining at Worms.

Specifically, the Calixtinum's provisions were: German episcopal and abbatial elections should take place at the imperial court. After a contested election in Germany, the emperor should support the "sounder part" *(sanior pars)* of the electors and the more suitable candidate; how-ever, the emperor's right to decide the dispute was further qualified by the provision that he should settle the conflict only after hearing the counsel and verdict of the metropolitan and the comprovincial bishops *(metropolitani et conprovincialium consilio vel iudicio)*. And with his scepter, the emperor should grant the *regalia* to German prelates-elect before their consecration. In Burgundy and Northern Italy, however, the *electus* should receive the *regalia* within the six months following his consecration; regalian investiture was thus relegated to a minor position in the non-German parts of the empire.

From a strict Gregorian viewpoint, election and consecration were the only two indispensable elements in the making of a bishop. As Geoffrey of Vendôme explained, the clergy are the vicars of Christ in the election of a bishop, the metropolitan and the other officiating bishops are the vicars of Christ in the consecration. This Gregorian emphasis on election and consecration implied, of course, the superfluousness of the monarch's investiture. Yet the Calixtinum assured Henry of a far-reaching authority over both election and consecration in Germany. The elections at the imperial court would inevitably be influenced by the emperor's wishes, and he had a decisive voice in any disputed election. Moreover, the emperor's investiture was to precede the consecration. With these concessions, therefore, Calixtus surrendered key points of the Gregorian program, and at least in Germany, the Concordat of Worms represents a limited victory for the emperor. Yet with its narrow provisions, the Concordat left many problems unsolved, and left much room for the free play of power. Even more clearly after Henry V's death in 1125, the relative power of the monarch was always a central factor determining his control over the promotions to the

German episcopate. Strong rulers, like Frederick Barbarossa and Henry VI, exerted a broad and not easily definable influence over German ecclesiastical elections. They went far beyond the rights explicitly conceded by the Calixtinum, and their sanctions derived from the custom and usage recognized by the imperial princes, rather than from a papal grant. On the other hand, the German monarchs of the thirteenth century were forced to abandon much of this imperial prerogative in episcopal elections.

Seen under the rubric of constitutional law rather than of politics, the Concordat left much room for a more detailed juridical definition of regalian investiture. Indeed, within the Concordat, the key term *regalia* was neither defined nor explained, but simply left to the reader's understanding. Informed contemporaries undoubtedly interpreted the term by reference to the more explicit documents of 1111. Nonetheless, the requirement of investiture before consecration constituted a kind of definition, for with the *regalia* the German *electus* won the right to receive his consecration. This requirement was, however, no radical innovation. Before 1122, the Concordat's prescribed sequence of investiture and consecration had been the normal practice in the empire, with the status of well-established custom—even though Paschal II had condemned it as "a custom intolerable to the Church." Moreover, a full generation before the Concordat, this prescribed sequence was already an articulate program, keynoted by imperialist forgers in the 1080's. Around 1100, Hugh of Fleury advocated the precedence of investiture before consecration, and imperialist pamphleteers of the early twelfth century echo the same refrain. In April 1111, when pope Paschal granted the "Pravilegium" to Henry V and recognized thereby the emperor's

prerogative in the elevation of bishops, the precedence of investiture appeared prominently among the pope's concessions. In this respect, then, the Concordat sanctioned and crystallized the existing policy and customary law of the empire, but did not create new law. Long after Henry V's death in 1125, this regulation was still considered binding in Germany. However, even in imperial circles, the Calixtinum was not regarded as the juridical basis for this requirement. Indeed, after Henry V's death, the Calixtinum was explicitly cited only once in support of imperial rights. Even in that one instance, Otto of Freising implies that the accepted custom of the imperial court was decisive for the precedence of investiture before consecration. For as the German bishops explained to the pope in the late twelfth century, immemorial tradition and the "approved usage" *(usus approbatus)* of Germany dictated the sequence of investiture and consecration. Any violation of this official sequence constituted, in their opinion, the "dismemberment" of the empire and the "utmost diminution of its rights.". . .

Throughout the twelfth century, the precedence of investiture remained a fundamental element of German customary law. Still, occasionally in the twelfth century and commonly in the thirteenth, a violation of this rule might provoke no reaction from the emperor. One may speculate that the chief cause of this indifference lay in the regulation itself, which related the investiture primarily to the prelate's consecration and hence to his sacramental powers. The main weakness of this rule—and the probable reason for its steadily lessening importance—was its failure to answer a central question: What powers does the investiture confer upon an *electus?*

The Calixtinum answered this question

straightforwardly: Calixtus's charter assured Henry that in Germany, each *"electus* should receive the *regalia* from you by way of the scepter." Indeed, this declaration clearly implied that the investiture conveys to the *electus* all of the powers and possessions summed up in the *regalia.* Yet Calixtus used precisely the same expression for the Burgundian and Italian bishops, who were to receive the investiture within six months of their consecration. It is hardly credible that these non-German bishops were expected to await a long deferred investiture before exercising their secular jurisdiction and administering their properties. Apparently, then, Calixtus's statement cannot be interpreted as a generally applicable stipulation that everywhere in the empire, the investiture effectively confers the *regalia,* and that before the investiture an *electus* may not administer his *regalia* in any way. In fact, it would not be easy to find among the eleventh-century sources an explicit and detailed assertion of such jurisdictional consequences for the act of investiture. Moreover, during the later eleventh and early twelfth centuries, it was possible to imagine an act of investiture without any juridically constitutive significance, that is, without any important effects. Cardinal Humbert had asserted—with indignation—that the prince's investiture conveys even the sacramental and purely ecclesiastical facets of the bishop's office, so that in the subsequent ecclesiastical investiture during the consecration, the metropolitan is performing a hollow ceremony. From a somewhat different point of view, when a later Gregorian claimed the Church's absolute rights over all properties ever conferred upon it, he concluded that any act of lay investiture therefore conveys nothing and is hence "superfluous and vain." Though both of these Gregorian doctrines denied the central

juridical meaning in the act, one was referring solely to ecclesiastical investiture, the other solely to lay investiture.

Nonetheless, for practical men, investiture meant the effective conveyance of properties and rights through a symbolic act of concession. And in eleventh-century imperial practice, the king's investiture was constitutive, for it formally inaugurated the new prelate into full possession of his jurisdictional and administrative powers. Moreover, eleventh-century usage was clearly reflected in the formula of investiture, as the king said to the future bishop, "Receive the church" *(Accipe ecclesiam).* Here the word *ecclesia* stands for the entire bishopric taken as a whole, without any distinction between office and property, between spiritual and temporal aspects. As eleventh-century Germany viewed the investiture, the entire office with all of its appurtenances—the *regimen pastorale* or *cura pastoralis* [pastoral rule or pastoral care]—was transferred when the crosier was handed over to the new prelate. Episcopal consecration was, of course, considered a necessity, but it added nothing to those governmental powers conferred on the bishop-elect at the moment of his investiture.

By 1100 the monarchists and the moderates of both camps were attempting to define, with a clarity and precision which had not previously been needed, the legal and constitutional significance of royal investiture. With their denial that this investiture confers any sacramental or spiritual prerogative, these theorists were forced to spell out the meaning of investiture, and to assert that the king's investiture is constitutive for the bishop-elect's power over his secular properties and jurisdiction. . . .

With only partial success, these theorists were trying to articulate the principle that investiture marks the effective beginning of the bishop-elect's regalian rights. An obvious corollary implied that prior to his investiture, a bishop-elect may not enter upon the powers and income from his *regalia*. Of course, imperial custom sanctioned these two principles, but as long as the lawfulness of investiture itself was in dispute, this aspect of custom could scarcely achieve the status of universally recognized law. . . .

To clarify the meaning of investiture was important. Yet the full value of a sharpened definition can be seen only against the background of contemporary Gregorian doctrine. Placidus of Nonantula must serve as the prime example, since he alone systematically elaborated the implications of the high Gregorian position on the problem of the *regalia*. Writing near the end of 1111, Placidus's thought reveals the extent to which the Church's property had become, for all parties, the key issue. As Placidus explained, the practice of investiture implies that the emperor has a proprietary right to the Church's possessions, and that a bishop cannot hold castles and lands unless he has received them "from the emperor's hand." Along similar lines, Placidus lucidly summarized the imperial claim that investiture is a constitutive act: "Without investiture, no one can have an ecclesiastical office and the worldly properties of his church." With equally acute perception, Placidus attacked the foundations of the imperial position. Since he believed that the emperor was categorically forbidden to invest churchmen, Placidus was obviously unwilling to admit that the emperor's investiture could be, in any respect, constitutive. Moreover, pointedly avoiding even the word *regalia*, Placidus refused to recognize a distinction between the *regalia* and any other properties or privileges pertaining to the Church. "Just as one

who separates the body from the soul destroys the man," he stated, "he who separates the *corporalia* from the *spiritualia* of a church destroys the church." Not only tithes and offerings, but also cities, castles, lands, even "dukeships and margraviates" and other secular offices belong to the Church as incontestable property. For "whatever has once been given to the Church belongs to Christ in perpetuity, nor can it in any way be alienated from the Church's possession." According to Placidus's system, when a bishop is consecrated, the metropolitan must invest the new bishop with the crosier, as a sign that the bishop has then received the lordship over the "worldly properties" *(terrenarum rerum dominium)* which his church possesses, and these "worldly properties" include everything which the emperor claimed as *regalia*. It is evident that in place of the constitutive investiture claimed by imperial custom and policy, Placidus has substituted a purely ecclesiastical investiture by the metropolitan. Yet for the new bishop, the metropolitan's investiture was constitutive only in a special and limited sense, since the bestowal of the crosier signified a divine bestowal of "worldly properties"; in Placidus's view, then, the new bishop actually received dominion over his temporal possessions "from the hand of the Lord." Indeed, within the ceremonial of an episcopal investiture and consecration, the metropolitan acts "in the place of Christ." Thus Placidus regarded the ecclesiastical investiture as primarily symbolic and declarative, but considered the divine conferment truly constitutive. There seems to be a contradiction, however, when Placidus observes in another passage that a bishop-elect must administer the properties of his church. With this remark, Placidus was apparently asserting that election, rather than ecclesiastical investiture or divine bestowal, was the constitutive moment. Yet Placidus's inconsistency does not affect the main point of his argument against the imperial conception of investiture. By either of Placidus's interpretations, the sanction for the administration of property lies with the Church, whether God and the metropolitan confer them in the investiture, or the clergy in the election. And in either case, there is no room for an imperial investiture. . . .

For compelling reasons, neither the supporters of the emperor nor the partisans of the papacy were truly satisfied with the Concordat of Worms. Shortly before the compromise of 1122, as Henry clung tenaciously to his time-honored right of investiture with ring and crosier, with unusual solidarity the secular princes of Germany had vigorously backed the emperor's claim, and had denounced their opponents as "wreckers." Nor did the agreement of 1122 really bring the Investiture Struggle to a decisive conclusion. Since investiture remained a live issue for more than a decade after 1122, in a literal sense the Investiture Struggle still continued. Indeed, even Lothar III, far more compliant than the three Henrys who preceded him, eventually proved reluctant to forget the valuable rights which Henry V had relinquished in the compromise of Worms. The newly elected Innocent II, driven from Rome by the supporters of the antipope Anacletus, met Lothar at Liège in March 1131, offered him the imperial coronation, and requested his help in expelling the "tyrant" from the Apostolic See. Lothar accepted this responsibility, and set in motion the machinery for an expedition to Italy, but he knew that his aid was indispensable—and he placed a high price upon it. For as Lothar explained to Innocent, his deep concern was "the ex-

tent to which the kingdom had been weakened by its love for the churches, and with how great a loss to itself it had surrendered their investiture." Since his own election in August 1125, there were undoubtedly incidents which convinced Lothar that the royal prerogative had been crippled by Henry V's concessions to the Church. For one thing, Lothar may have been unable to prevent the election of hostile prelates in Germany. Equally dangerous were the possible violations directed against his royal right of investiture: either consecration before investiture, or seizure of the *regalia* before investiture. In fact, however, there is no positive evidence that any such incidents occurred between August 1125 and March 1131. Whatever the specific symptoms were at Liège King Lothar proposed a strong remedy:

Thinking that he had an opportune time, the king stubbornly insisted that the investiture of bishops, which the Roman Church had taken away from his predecessor . . . with the greatest efforts and many dangers, should be restored to himself.

In effect, Lothar was demanding the restoration of the pre-1122 form of investiture: that is, the reestablishment of investiture with ring and staff. Badly frightened, Innocent and his retinue were saved from Lothar's importunity only by the eloquent intervention of St. Bernard.

In the two years following the meeting at Liège, Lothar had ample chance to reflect that his relations with the German episcopate were deteriorating further. During that period an archbishop of Trier and a bishop of Regensburg—and perhaps other German prelates as well—received the episcopal consecration before the regalian investiture. On both occasions the new prelates had also administered the *regalia* prior to the investiture. It was clear that the pope and a part of the German episcopate were prepared simply to ignore the customary law of the empire. Moreover, it was obvious that if these violations became common in Germany, they would soon transform the investiture into a meaningless formality there, just as in Italy. Lothar was in a serious predicament, for he was personally "devoted to the rights of the Church," and he owed his royal election in large part to German ecclesiastical princes. Consequently, he was neither temperamentally inclined nor politically able to conduct an all-out struggle against the papacy and the recusant prelates. In addition, by the time of his imperial coronation on 4 June 1133, Lothar was closely tied to Innocent by a group of far-reaching agreements which a contemporary accurately described as a "treaty" *(foedus)*. Lothar had already promised his help against Innocent's rival, and in his imperial coronation oath he solemnized his obligation to Innocent and the Roman Church. For his own part, Innocent conferred the imperial crown on Lothar. Of mutual advantage was Innocent's investiture of Lothar with the Tuscan patrimony of the countess Matilda. However, when Innocent granted to Magdeburg and to Hamburg-Bremen full recognition of their old claims to jurisdiction over neighboring non-German dioceses, his measures primarily rewarded Norbert of Magdeburg and Adalbero of Hamburg-Bremen for their loyalty, rather than Lothar for his services. In general, these various concessions and agreements may well have seemed to Lothar one-sided, and they certainly did not materially help his position in relation to the ecclesiastical princes of Germany. Immediately after his imperial coronation, therefore, Lothar repeated the stipulation made two years earlier at Liège:

Crowned . . . in confirmation of the treaty which he had concluded with the pope, the emperor rashly demanded that the investiture of bishoprics—in other words, the liberty of the churches—should be relinquished to him by the lord pope.

Once again, Lothar was demanding the restoration of investiture with ring and staff; for the second time, he sought to nullify the central provision in Henry V's concession of 1122. Lothar had rightly assessed the weaknesses of Innocent's character and of his political position. Precariously holding only a part of Rome, the hard-pressed pontiff still needed his "treaty" with Lothar, and he was on the point of granting Lothar's demand. Nonetheless, Lothar's policy reveals a certain political naïveté, for even if Innocent had yielded, his decree could scarcely have been enforced against the inevitable opposition of German prelates like Adalbert of Mainz and Conrad of Salzburg. It was fortunate for everyone, therefore, when once again an influential churchman intervened to rescue the hesitant pope—this time, archbishop Norbert of Magdeburg, who stiffened the pope's resistance and dissuaded the emperor from his stand. In principle, however, archbishop Norbert was not opposed to imperial influence in the elevation of bishops, and he may well have negotiated the ensuing compromise between Lothar and Innocent: Four days after the imperial coronation, the pope granted Lothar a charter dealing with the question of regalian investiture, and thereby Innocent made a major addition to the "treaty" between the emperor and himself. After this concordat of June 1133, the issue of investiture with ring and crosier never reappeared in the relations between papacy and empire.

In this papal privilege of 1133, the wording is as careful and cautious as in

Calixtus II's charter for Henry V, for like the Calixtinum, Innocent II's grant was personal in form, valid for Lothar's lifetime but not intended for his successors. Though Innocent's assurances to Lothar were clothed in ambiguity, at first glance they seem perfectly fashioned as vague expressions of benign intent toward the emperor. Praising Lothar for his devotion to the Church and for his opposition to the antipope, Innocent announced that in the coronation he was conceding to Lothar "the fullness of the imperial office":

Wishing, therefore, not to diminish but to increase the majesty of the *imperium,* we grant you the fullness of the imperial office, and by these presents, we confirm the required and canonical customs.

At the very least, Innocent was here emphasizing the value of the imperial coronation, and the importance of his own role as bestower of the imperial title. Within these resounding phrases, however, there was grave danger for the theoretical position of the emperor. Innocent's language was strikingly different from Paschal II's restrained statement in 1111, when he asserted that "through the ministry of our priesthood, the Divine Majesty" had elevated Henry V to the imperial dignity. By claiming that he himself was granting "the fullness of the imperial office," Innocent almost maintained that the imperial coronation was a constitutive act, in which the Roman pontiff conferred an office together with all of its powers. Moreover, some may have sensed the resemblance between Innocent's term, the *imperatoriae dignitatis plenitudo* [fullness of the imperial dignity], and the contemporary expression *plenitudo officii pontificalis* [fullness of the pontifical office], which summarized the powers granted to an archbishop-elect with the bestowal of the *pallium.* In Innocent's

charter, however, the claim is partly veiled, the language is far from explicit and the threat is latent. Yet it is significant that Innocent's term reappeared twenty-four years later, in the famous incident at Besançon, when Hadrian IV enraged the imperial princes with his statement that in Barbarossa's imperial coronation, the Roman See had conferred the *plenitudo dignitatis* [fullness of the dignity] on him.

Even more indefinite was Innocent's confirmation of "the required and canonical customs." Here, Innocent was surely referring to the emperor's relations with the German church, but by simply guaranteeing these "customs" without explanation of their nature, he carefully avoided making a specific commitment to Lothar. Indeed, with this expression, the pontiff did not even expressly renew the provisions of the Calixtinum, much less turn back the clock to the constitutional practices of an earlier age. Rather, Innocent merely promised just treatment, suitable to the properly precedented rights of the imperial office in its relation to the German church. Innocent himself may well have held a strict and antimonarchical conception of these "canonical customs." Nonetheless, it is clear that in the opinion of Lothar and most German bishops, a papal confirmation of "the required and canonical customs" would imply the ratification of one of the usages formerly prescribed by the Calixtinum, since customary practice in Germany still required investiture as the normal prerequisite to consecration.

But in its final sentence, Innocent's charter went far beyond the Calixtinum, for it brought a valuable new concession: a stipulation that no one who is elevated to the episcopal or abbatial office in Germany "should dare to usurp or to seize the *regalia*" before having requested them from Lothar. Here Innocent's diction is no less obscure than in his assurances on "the fullness of the imperial office" and on "the required and canonical customs." Though the Calixtinum had specifically referred to the investiture of an *electus,* the Innocentianum used a clumsy circumlocution in order to avoid this expression; thereby, Innocent left the sequence of investiture and consecration unclear. Equally obscure is Innocent's statement that the new prelate must "request" *(deposcere)* the *regalia.* Did Innocent mean to imply that a mere request by a prelate is sufficient warrant for seizure and administration of the *regalia?* In fact, the document ignores the question of the emperor's right to refuse the prelate's request for the *regalia,* and it by-passes the corollary question of the prelate's rights in the event of such a refusal. Yet the ambiguities in the Innocentianum were a matter of policy. Indeed, a comparison of Innocent's charter with earlier papal documents on investiture shows unmistakably that the papal chancery composed this grant with earlier usage in mind. It is, of course, obvious that the Innocentianum was the product of hard negotiation. Presumably, therefore, in this charter Innocent had made his maximum concessions, and Lothar's minimum conditions had been met.

In general, then, the charter's murky diction reveals the papacy's determination not to revalidate the Calixtinum, and to yield as little as possible in the crucial question of investiture. Through such deliberate obscurities, the papacy had guarded itself, for a strict Curialist interpretation of Innocent's charter could vastly reduce its value to Lothar. Still, despite the careful ambiguities of the papal chancery, it is clear that in the practical thinking of the imperial court, the Innocentianum would be interpreted as a simple and straightforward prohibition, categorically forbidding any German bishop-elect to administer his temporalities prior to his investiture. The tangible consequences of this restriction were serious, for without his investiture, a German prelate-elect could neither exercise his secular jurisdiction, nor command his vassals, nor enjoy the income from the regalian properties attached to his office and his church. Lothar gained more from this requirement than he would have won from papal recognition of investiture as a necessary prerequisite to consecration. Far more clearly than the Calixtinum, the Innocentianum explicitly recognized and protected a crucial element of the royal prerogative: the monarch's proprietary claim to the *regalia.* Although Lothar's original demand at Rome was refused, Innocent's grant was a substitute which could serve as a powerful safeguard against any future violations like the recent ones at Trier and Regensburg.

In defining the juridical content of investiture, the Roman concordat of 1133 was explicitly valid only for the kingdom of Germany. This fact implied a further widening of the growing gulf between the constitutional position of the German episcopate and that of the episcopate in the other two kingdoms of the empire. Of course, the differences between conditions in Germany and in the rest of the empire had long existed, and had been formalized in the Concordat of Worms. Moreover, as we have seen, the concordat of 1133 did not alter the customary sequence of investiture and consecration, either in the German bishoprics or elsewhere. Indeed, it was silent on that question. Rather, within Germany, the Roman concordat ratified a *second* function of investiture as a prerequisite to the administration of the *regalia* as well as to the episcopal consecration.

Even though the Innocentianum defined the constitutive effects of regalian investiture, it did not truly give new juridical significance to that act, nor impose a new requirement upon the German bishops. Rather, this regulation had deep roots in the German past, for long before the concordats of 1122 and 1133, it was a standard part of imperial practice. Indeed, this rule was an object of negotiation in 1111, and it had been assumed in more than one publicistic treatise. Because the regulation already belonged to imperial public law, it did not depend upon the Innocentianum. Strictly speaking, therefore, Lothar had small reason to regret that the Innocentianum was granted to himself personally and not to his successors, for he could be confident that this crucial requirement would outlast the Innocentianum. Still, by providing a papal guarantee of a traditional regulation, the Innocentianum strengthened its legal foundations at a moment when they were visibly crumbling. Since the ecclesiastical princes of Germany were subject to the Roman See as well as to imperial law, the authority of the papacy was now added to the force of imperial custom. After 1133, Church and papacy had to recognize that this regulation was, so to speak, one of "the required and canonical customs."

ARNOLD J. TOYNBEE (b. 1889) is one of the most versatile and prolific historians of the present day. His multivolume *A Study of History*, a vast analytic typology of all the world's historical civilizations, crowned a career that included teaching classical and Byzantine Greek literature, directing studies in the Royal Institute of International Affairs (1925–1955), and negotiating as a member of the British delegations at two Paris Peace Conferences (1919, 1946). Despite the duties of public service, Toynbee has written extensively on many subjects, including recent Greek, Turkish, and Near Eastern affairs. His encyclopedic knowledge of world history and his participation in current diplomacy at the highest level convinced Toynbee that resort to arms marked a downward swerve in the course of any civilization or institution, and that a world empire built up by war signaled a civilization's breakdown. This view molded his understanding of the Investiture Controversy's long-range effects.*

Arnold J. Toynbee

The Downfall of the Papacy

Note by Arnold Toynbee, from whose book, A Study of History, *the following extracts have been taken with the permission of the author himself and his publishers, the Oxford University Press, London and New York*

Mr. Toynbee and his publishers have much appreciated Professor Morrison's wish to include the following passages of *A Study of History* in the present book, and they have been glad to give their permission. At the same time, Mr. Toynbee asks the readers of the present book to bear in mind the following points: (i) the volume of Mr. Toynbee's from which these extracts have been taken was published as long ago as 1939; (ii) this does not make these passages obsolete; the Middle Ages are still what they were in 1939; (iii) but, since 1939, a new chapter in the history of the Papacy has opened; (iv) some of the issues that were controversial in the eleventh and twelfth centuries have become controversial once more, but on different terms.

Today the question of the celibacy of the clergy is not being raised, as it was in the eleventh century, by a scandalous prevalence of concubinage. The question today is whether, for priests, celibacy is a good or a bad thing in itself. Is it good or bad for priests themselves as human beings? Does it help them or hinder them in performing their service for

*From *A Study of History,* Volume IV, by Arnold J. Toynbee, published by the Oxford University Press for the Royal Institute of International Affairs. Printed in 1939. Pp. 512–514, 551–557, 532–538, 544–547, 576–584. Footnotes omitted.

the laity? Today celibacy is not a remedy for misconduct, as it was in the eleventh century.

Today again, the issue over Papal authority is not the question whether the Pope is justified in using physical force (this is now neither conceivable nor practicable). Nor is it just a question of determining where the dividing line should be drawn between the respective fields of ecclesiastical and secular authority. Papal authority itself is now in question.

Mr. Toynbee hopes that present-day readers of these extracts from a book of his that was published more than thirty years ago will recognise that these passages are not concerned with controversies that have arisen subsequently. The judgments that, in these passages, Mr. Toynbee has expressed about previous chapters of the history of the Papacy may be right or wrong, but in any case they are not his judgments on the present chapter.

* * *

Perhaps the most signal of all public examples of the disastrous consequences of the intoxication of victory is afforded by one of the chapters in the long, and still living and lengthening, history of the Papacy.

The chapter in the history of this greatest of all Western institutions which began on the 20th December, 1046, with the opening of the Synod of Sutri by the Emperor Henry III, and which closed on the 20th September, 1870, with the occupation of Rome by the troops of King Victor Emmanuel, displays certain broad correspondences with a chapter of almost equal length in the history of the Roman Republic which began with the *Clades Alliensis* [Celtic sack of Rome] of the 18th July, 390 B.C., and closed with the occupation of Rome by Alaric on the 24th August, A.D. 410. In both these dramas the wheel comes round full circle. In the historical tragedy of Papal Rome the ecclesiastical head of Western Christendom was compelled twice over to capitulate in his own See to a secular sovereign, as in

the tragedy of pagan Rome the city which was the warden of the continental European marches of the Hellenic World was likewise compelled twice over to admit a barbarian trespasser within her walls. In both these chapters of history the period of more than eight hundred years which the wheel of Fortune took to revolve was occupied by an extraordinary feat and an extraordinary fall. And in both chapters Rome brought her fall upon herself.

Without elaborating our parallel too fancifully, we may notice how these two versions of the Roman tragedy resemble one another act by act.

Just as the *Clades Alliensis* evoked among the citizens of the Roman Republic the mood in which, half a century later, they contended with the Samnites for the hegemony of Italy and won the prize through their victory in a fifty years' war (343–290 B.C.), so the blow dealt to the Papacy by the Emperor Henry III at the Synod of Sutri reverberated in the soul of Hildebrand for thirty years until he threw down the gauntlet to the Emperor Henry IV and launched the Papacy on its fifty years' contest with the Empire over the question of Investiture (A.D. 1075–1122). And if the conflict between the Papacy and the Salian Dynasty is comparable to the warfare between Rome and Samnium, the more violent, bitter, and devastating conflict between the Papacy and the Hohenstaufen Dynasty is still more strikingly reminiscent of the warfare between Rome and Carthage. In either case the duel between Rome and her arch-enemy took three rounds to fight itself out; and each successive round was fought with greater savagery than its predecessor. If the struggles between Pope Alexander III and the Emperor Frederick I, and between Pope Gregory IX and the Emperor Frederick II, may be regarded as the respective analogues of the First and

Second Romano-Punic wars, the spirit in which the Romans made the Third Romano-Punic War, with the deliberate purpose of annihilating in cold blood an enemy who was already prostrate, was unmistakably revived in the Catonian implacability with which an Innocent IV and an Urban IV kept up their feud with the Emperor Frederick II after their great enemy's death, and insisted upon converting it from a quarrel with a single individual into a vendetta which could not be appeased by any lesser retribution than the complete ruin and annihilation of the whole of the offender's house.

In this Hohenstaufen-Punic act of the twice-performed Roman play the resemblances even extend to details. For example, the strategy of Frederick Barbarossa after his acknowledgement, in the peace-treaties of Venice (A.D. 1177) and Constance (A.D. 1183), of his failure to reassert the Imperial authority in Lombardy may be compared with Hamilcar Barca's strategy after the cession of the old Carthaginian dominion in Sicily in the peace settlement of 241 B.C. As Hamilcar set himself to conquer for Carthage a new and more valuable empire in the Iberian Peninsula, so Frederick secured for the House of Hohenstaufen the reversion of the Kingdom of Sicily. In either case a Power which had just been foiled in one trial of strength with its Roman adversary proceeded to occupy a new coign of vantage from which it could attack Rome on a second front with fresh supplies of men and money. In either case the consequence of this masterly stroke on the part of Rome's opponent was a second trial of strength on a greater scale which ended in confirming Rome's victory, but which brought her, first, so near to defeat, and left the victor's heart so morbidly obsessed by fear and hatred of the vanquished, that Rome could not rest until she had

returned to the attack and had dealt her already beaten and stricken enemy "the knock-out blow."

In the next act a victorious Rome collapses ignominiously under the weight of a vindictiveness which has led her to pursue her adversary's destruction to her own undoing. The century of humiliation (A.D. 1303–1418) which was the nemesis of the Papacy's relentless pursuit of its vendetta against the Hohenstaufen has its analogue in the century of suffering with which the Roman Republic had to pay for the cold-blooded destruction of Carthage. The desecration of the Pope's personal sacrosanctity through the brutal handling of Boniface VIII by Guillaume Nogaret and Sciarra Colonna may be compared with the pricking of the bubble of Roman military prestige by the ignominy of Mancinus's capitulation to the Numantines. In the sequel "the Babylonish captivity" of the Papacy may be compared with the bout of revolution into which the Republic fell in 133 B.C., and "the Great Schism" with the civil war out of which the Empire emerged in 31 B.C.

In either version, again, the last act is a melancholy and tedious anti-climax in which the play drags on for some four centuries longer before the curtain descends. If we fix our attention upon the abortive rallies by which the gloom of this twilight age is partially relieved, we may discern a dim resemblance between the pontificate of Martin V and the principate of Augustus and between "the Counter-Reformation" and "the Indian Summer" of the Antonines. And as we watch the last scene of all we may detect in Pope Pius IX, who became "the prisoner in the Vatican" as soon as the French garrison withdrew from Rome and the Italian army marched in, an historical counterpart of the Emperor Honorius, who became "the refugee in Ravenna" when

Rome was left at Alaric's mercy by the removal of Stilicho's protecting hand. . . .

In Hildebrand's generation the Western Christendom was passing out of the first into the second chapter of its history —out of a defensive state of mind in which the height of ambition was to keep alive, as the Abbé Siéyès boasted in a later age that he had lived through the French Revolution, into an adventurous state of mind in which this vegetative life for life's sake began to seem hardly worth living unless it could now be transcended, on the Aristotelian scheme of social growth, in an effort to make life a stepping-stone towards attaining the true end of Man. This troubling of the waters of Western life in the eleventh century of the Christian Era revealed itself most powerfully in a mighty movement for reforming the conduct of the Church, which in that age was another name for the Western Society itself; and this movement presented a challenge to the Roman See because, in the relations between the Papacy and the Western body social, it made it impossible for the *status quo ante* to persist. It was only in a society that was numb with misery—as Western Christendom had been from the twilight of Charlemagne's generation to the dawn of Otto the Great's—that the prerogative of moral leadership could be left, even nominally, in the hands of an institution which was disgracing itself as the Roman See disgraced itself during that profligate passage in its history. From the moment when the Western World as a whole began to shake off its moral torpor and aspire to a better life, the Roman See was confronted with the alternative of leaping at one bound from the lowest to the highest rung of the moral ladder as it stood in that age, or else being pilloried in its actual state of degradation and seeing its

kingdom numbered and finished and divided and given to the Medes and Persians. There was a danger-signal for discerning eyes in the Lateran in the tremor of indignation which ran through Western Christendom—and with particular vehemence in the Transalpine parts— when it was reported in 1024 that the Greeks were in negotiation with the Papacy for the purchase of Papal acquiescence in the Patriarch of Constantinople's long-maintained and long-contested pretension to the title of "Oecumenical." This explosion of anger at an only too credible rumour that the Pope was selling his birthright for a mess of pottage showed that the profligacy of the Roman See was notorious and odious to the Western *Plebs Christiana* [Christian People]. And when, a score of years later, the Papal *capellanus* [Chaplain] Hildebrand, in whose own soul the spirit of the age was working, saw an Emperor conduct the trial and procure the condemnation of a Pope on a charge of Simony, he read the meaning of this writing on the wall and went into action. In that hour Hildebrand set himself the tremendous task of reversing the judgement upon the Roman See which had just been pronounced at Sutri; and in thirty years of titanic labour he succeeded in achieving the impossible. By 1075 the double battle against the sexual and the financial corruption of the clergy had been won throughout the Western World, and the victory had been gained by the moral prowess of a Roman See whose profligacy had been the greatest of all the scandals of the Western Church in the preceding century. This victory had been Hildebrand's personal work. He had fought for it beyond the Alps and behind the Papal Throne until the fight had carried him at last into the office which he had raised from the dust; and he had fought with every weapon, spiritual or material, that had come to his hand. It was at the moment of triumph, in the third year of his reign as Pope Gregory VII, that Hildebrand took a step which his champions can plausibly represent as having been almost inevitable and his critics—no less plausibly—as having been almost inevitably disastrous. In that year Hildebrand extended his field of battle from the sure ground of Concubinage and Simony to the debatable ground of Investiture.

Logically, perhaps, the conflict over Investiture might be justified as an inevitable sequel to the conflicts over Concubinage and Simony if all three struggles were looked upon as aspects of one single struggle for the liberation of the Church. To a Hildebrand at this critical point in his career it might almost seem labour lost to have freed the Church from her servitude to Venus and to Mammon, if he were to leave her still fettered by her political subjection to the Secular Power. So long as this third shackle lay heavy upon her, would she not still be debarred from doing her divinely appointed work for the regeneration of Mankind? This argument on the lips of the apologists for Hildebrand's new departure in the year 1075 begs a question which Hildebrand's critics are entitled to ask, even if they fail to prove conclusively that the answer to it is in their own favour. In A.D. 1075, were the circumstances such that any clear-sighted and strong-minded occupant of the Papal throne was bound to judge that there was no longer any possibility of sincere and fruitful co-operation between the reforming party in the Western Church, as represented by the Roman Curia, and the Secular Power in the Western Christian Commonwealth, as represented by the Holy Roman Empire? On this question the onus of proof lies with the Hildebrandines on at least two accounts.

In the first place neither Hildebrand himself nor his partisans ever sought—either before or after the promulgation of Hildebrand's decree prohibiting Lay Investiture in 1075—to deny that the secular authorities had a legitimate role to play in the procedure for the election of the clerical officers of the Church from the Pope himself downwards. In the second place, within the thirty years ending in 1075 the Roman See had been working hand in hand with the Holy Roman Empire in the older conflict over the issues of Concubinage and Simony. Indeed, their co-operation had become so sincere and so cordial that the Emperor Henry III, who had forced Pope Gregory VI out of office and into exile in 1046, chose Pope Victor II ten years later, when the the Emperor was on his deathbed, to be the guardian of his six-year-old son. It is true that, in the domain of the Empire, if not in the Western World as a whole, Henry III's premature death in A.D. 1056 had been followed by a moral relapse—especially in the matter of Simony—which had begun during the minority of Henry III's namesake and son and successor Henry IV and had not ceased when the young prince had taken over the reins of government himself in A.D. 1069. In fact, "behind any particular occasions of difference there lay a more general cause, and this was the fact that after the death of Henry III the temporal authority was no longer co-operating with the spiritual in the attempt at reform, but seemed rather to be responsible for the continuance of grave evils, such as Simony and the secularization of the clergy. It was under these circumstances that the Papacy began to develop the policy of limiting or prohibiting the intervention of the secular authority in ecclesiastical appointments. This may have been justifiable and even necessary, but it must be admitted that it was a step of an almost revolutionary character", and if, in spite of all justifications and provocations, Hildebrand had foreborne to throw down the gauntlet in A.D. 1075, it is conceivable that the relations of the Emperor Henry IV with Pope Gregory might have ended in being not less happy than his father's relations with Pope Victor.

To raise the new issue of Investiture with a militancy which was bound to set Empire and Papacy at variance was the more hazardous inasmuch as this third issue happened to be far less clear than those others on which the two authorities in Western Christendom had, not so long since, seen eye to eye.

One source of ambiguity arose from the fact that, by Hildebrand's day, it had become established that the appointment of a clerical officer of episcopal rank required, in order to make it valid, the concurrence of several different parties in taking action of several different kinds. It was one of the primeval rules of ecclesiastical discipline that a bishop must be elected by the clergy and people of his see and must be consecrated by a quorum of the validly consecrated bishops of the province. And the secular power had never at any time—since the issue had been raised by the conversion of Constantine—attempted to usurp the ritual prerogative of the bishops or to challenge, at any rate in theory, the electoral rights of the clergy and people. The role which the secular authorities had exercised *de facto*—without prejudice to the question of what the situation might be *de jure*—was that of nominating candidates and wielding a power of veto over elections; and this power, which was grounded

in Roman Imperial practice, had been successfully reasserted in the West by the Holy Roman Emperors Charlemagne and Otto I, in anticipation of Henry III, against the Papacy itself, which was the highest ecclesiastical office in the Western World. There may be some uncertainty about the scope of the powers which, on the morrow of the Synod of Sutri, were conferred upon Henry as *patricius* by the Roman clergy and people; but it is certain that the first step in the making of a Pope Leo IX out of a Bruno Bishop of Toul, and of a Pope Victor II out of a Gebhard Bishop of Eichstett, was the despatch of a diplomatic mission across the Alps from Rome to the Emperor to ask for an Imperial nomination; and in the second of these instances the Roman mission came with Hildebrand at its head. Even as late as the year 1059, after Henry's death, Hildebrand took care to obtain the assent of the Empress Regent before he gave his own support to the candidature of Gerard Bishop of Florence; and at the famous Lateran Council which was held in the same year by Hildebrand's candidate after he had been duly elected to be Pope Nicholas II, when the Fathers laid down a procedure for Papal elections in the future, the Emperor's rights in the matter were once again formally acknowledged, even though they were left undefined. If the traditional role of the Secular Power in the appointment of the highest ecclesiastical dignitary in the West was as substantial as this, the case for the exercise of a corresponding lay influence over the appointment of ordinary bishops and abbots might almost be taken as proven *a fortiori,* and it is not certain that the legitimacy of this influence, within its traditional limits, was disputed by Hildebrand even after the promulgation of the decree of 1075.

This uncertainty arises out of a second ambiguity which is of a verbal order and which "runs through the whole literature of the subject." The word "Investiture" is ambiguous in itself. It may be used in the general meaning of appointment, or in the technical meaning of the bestowal of the pastoral staff and ring. And an opponent of Lay Investiture may be opposing the practice in this narrow technical sense without necessarily at the same time seeking to exclude the secular authorities from influencing appointments to clerical offices in the traditional ways.

By the eleventh century the traditional case for the exercise of some degree of secular control over clerical appointments had been reinforced by a new consideration of a practical kind which likewise applied to the lower ranks as well as to the apex of the Western hierarchy and which introduced yet a third ambiguity into an already complicated problem. This third ambiguity lay in the matter of the clergy's functions. The "Caesaro-papistical" thesis manifestly gains in strength if the clergy over whom the secular power claims to exercise control become possessed, on their part, of secular as well as ecclesiastical emoluments and authority; and this had actually been happening all over Western Christendom during the three centuries ending in the reign of the Emperor Henry III. The donations of Pepin and Charlemagne to the Papacy were merely the classical examples of a widespread transfer, into clerical hands, of the civil power's *regalia;* and this oecumenical secular movement had been at no time so active as during the two centuries between the death of Charlemagne and the birth of Hildebrand. By the year 1075, when Hildebrand launched his campaign against the Lay Investiture of clerics, a very large part of the civil administration of Western Christendom was in the hands of clerics who held it as of feudal right, so that the exemption of the clergy from Lay Investiture in the broader sense would now carry with it an abrogation of the Secular Power's authority over large tracts of its own proper field and a transformation of the Church into a civil as well as an ecclesiastical *imperium in imperio* [empire inside an empire]. To demand this—if Hildebrand did unequivocally demand so much—was to declare war; and, if we ask ourselves what can have led so great a man as Hildebrand to take so grave a step, the most convincing answer will be that his judgement was clouded on this critical occasion by the intoxicating consciousness of his previous triumphs. "All things are possible to him that believeth" is a dangerous text for a human being to act upon, even when the man is a Gregory VII.

The gravity of Hildebrand's action in 1075 is revealed by the dimensions of the catastrophe which was its sequel. On this issue of Investiture Hildebrand staked the whole of the moral prestige which he had won for the Papacy in thirty years; and his hold upon the consciences of the *Plebs Christiana* in Henry IV's Transalpine dominions was strong enough, in conjunction with the strength of Saxon arms, to bring the Emperor to Canossa. Yet, although Canossa may have dealt the Imperial dignity a blow from which it perhaps never quite recovered, the sequel to that moral triumph was not an end, but a resumption, of the struggle which Hildebrand had let loose two years before. The end was not brought even by Paschal II's fundamental but abortive settlement with Henry IV's son and namesake in 1111, nor again by Calixtus II's successful but superficial settlement with the same Emperor in 1122; for, although the question of Investiture was officially disposed of by the Concordat of Worms, those fifty years of conflict had produced a rift between the Papacy and the Empire which might perhaps be precariously bridged but which was now too wide to be closed and too deep to be filled. When a Frederick I succeeded to the heritage of the Henrys and was armed, by Bolognese doctors of the disinterred *Corpus Juris,* with a Justinianean conception of the Imperial prerogative to match the Hildebrandine conception of the Apostolic power, the unhealed wound in the Western body social broke open again, and the new Justinian's battle with an ineffective Hadrian IV and an indomitable Alexander III reproduced the battle that had been fought by his predecessor Henry V with a saintly Paschal and a masterful Calixtus. The fire which Hildebrand had kindled in 1075 was still burning fiercely a hundred years later. . . .

The medieval Papacy, like the modern English governing class and the Ottoman Pādishāh's Slave-Household, had the power of attracting into its service all the talents of the society in which it was the master-institution. The Hildebrandine Church knew how to use an extraordinary variety of aptitudes and experiences in a cause which was so much vaster and so much grander than the *raison d'être* of any national state or multi-national empire. A closer scrutiny will show that these diverse types of eminence were not all equally apt for doing the precise and special work of controlling the destinies of the Christian Republic through the instrumentality of the Roman Curia. The fortunes of a Gregory VI or a Paschal II — not to speak of Celestine V — suggest that a man who was eminent as an unworldly saint would perhaps find himself at a disadvantage on the Papal throne, where he might be hindered by his office from exercising his gifts and be hampered by

his gifts from fulfilling his office. When we compare the respective results of a Paschal II's and a Calixtus II's dealings with a Henry V, we may be inclined to think that the virtues of a saint were a less valuable endowment than the family tradition of a sovereign count for a Pope who was called upon to live up to the Hildebrandine faith that God had

made him lord of his house and ruler of all his substance,
To bind his princes at his pleasure and teach his senators wisdom.

A count in Pope's clothing, like Calixtus II or Eugenius III, might be the most effective vicegerent of God for calling to order a prince like the aggressive Emperor Henry V or a senator like the turbulent revolutionary Arnold of Brescia. If the capable and commanding nobleman were, as Eugenius was, a monk and a saint besides, so much greater the edification; but, for the service of the Holy See, the nobleman's qualities were perhaps more important; and, to judge by the prowess of Alexander III in fighting his desperate battle with Frederick I, the qualities of the lawyer were even more valuable than those of the nobleman for waging the warfare of the Church Militant. It was perhaps better still to combine the lawyer's cutting edge with the nobleman's robust self-assurance; for this was the combination of worldly gifts which triumphed, in an Innocent IV and a Clement IV, over the demonic energies of Frederick II and his offspring. If we follow our argument as far as this, however, we shall find ourselves in deep waters; for Boniface VIII was a nobly born lawyer likewise; and it was Boniface's infatuation that brought down the whole magnificent structure of the Papal *Respublica Christiana* [Christian commonwealth] with a crash, to lie in ruins side by side with that Holy Roman Empire which had been shattered, less than half a century back, by an Innocent's implacability. These two stiff-necked and self-confident men of the world, with their aristocratic imperiousness and their legal exactingness, did far more than the soft-hearted and incompetent Abruzzese peasant's son to destroy all that had been built up by Pope after Pope for two centuries on end upon the Hildebrandine foundations.

If Hildebrand himself on his death-bed could have confronted, with foreknowledge of the event, the long array of his coming successors, he would assuredly have cried out, in his Master's words, "verily I say unto you that one of you shall betray me," and the only plea that could have been offered in self-defence by a then unborn Benedetto Gaetani or Sinibaldo Fieschi would have been that his future betrayal of Hildebrand was already predetermined by Hildebrand's own betrayal of himself. Our catalogue of great Popes, from Gregory VII to Boniface VIII inclusive, proclaims that the elements of greatness which created the Papal *Respublica Christiana* were also the elements that destroyed it, and that these seeds of destruction were being sown from the outset.

The fall of the Hildebrandine Church is as extraordinary a spectacle as its rise; for all the virtues that had carried it to its zenith seem to change, as it sinks to its nadir, into their own exact antitheses. The divine institution which had been fighting and winning a battle for spiritual freedom against material force was now infected with the very evil which it had set itself to cast out from the body social of Western Christendom. The Holy See which had taken the lead in the struggle against simony now required the clergy throughout the Western World to pay their dues at a Roman receipt of custom for those ecclesiastical preferments which

Rome herself had forbidden them to purchase from any local secular power. The Roman Curia which had been the head and front of moral and intellectual progress—a tower of strength for the saints who were raising the monastic life to new heights, and for the schoolmen who were creating the universities—now turned itself into a fastness of spiritual conservatism. The ecclesiastical sovereign power in the Christian Republic now suffered itself to be deprived by its local secular underlings—the princes of the rising parochial states of Western Christendom—of the lion's share of the product of financial and administrative instruments which the Papacy itself had skilfully devised in order to make its authority effective; and this forfeiture of a share in the product was followed by a forfeiture of the means of production as well when in England a King Henry VIII took over the Papal machinery within the frontiers of his own realm and thenceforward worked the machine with his own hands for his own profit exclusively. In the face of this final act of spoliation the Holy See found itself helpless. And as the local prince of a Papal principality the Sovereign Pontiff eventually had to content himself—like Napoleon on Elba—with the paltry consolation-prize of sovereignty over one of the least of the "successor-states" of his own lost empire. Has any other institution ever given so great occasion as this to the enemies of the Lord to blaspheme? The downfall of the Hildebrandine Papacy is a more extreme case of περιπέτεια [sudden change of fortune, as in a tragedy] than any that we have yet encountered in our study of the nemesis of creativity. How did it happen, and why?

How it happened is foreshadowed in the first recorded transaction in Hildebrand's public career.

The creative spirits in the Roman Church who set themselves in the eleventh century to rescue our Western World from a feudal anarchy by establishing a Christian Republic then found themselves in the same dilemma as their spiritual heirs who are attempting in our day to replace an international anarchy by a political world order. The essence of their aim was to substitute a reign of spiritual authority for the reign of physical force, and in their struggle against violence the spiritual sword was the weapon with which their supreme victories were won. No physical force was exerted in Hildebrand's act of deposing and excommunicating the Emperor Henry IV; yet the moral effect of the Pope's winged words upon the hearts of the Emperor's Transalpine subjects was so intense that within a few months it brought Henry to Canossa. There were, however, other occasions on which it seemed as though the established regime of physical force was in a position to defy the strokes of the spiritual sword with impunity; and it was in such situations that the Roman Church Militant was challenged to give its answer to the Riddle of the Sphinx. Was the soldier of God to deny himself the use of any but his own spiritual arms, at the risk of seeing his advance brought to a standstill? Or was he to fight God's battle against the Devil with the adversary's own weapons, if the only practicable way of ejecting the adversary from his entrenchments was to hoist him with his own petard? Which was the true Christian act of faith? To eschew all weapons but God's, and trust in God to make David's sling prevail against Goliath's panoply? Or to remind himself that the Devil and his armoury, like everything else in the Universe, were the Creator's creatures, and to believe that no created thing could remain unhallowed if it were used in the Creator's

service? "What God hath cleansed, that call not thou common" was a text which might appear to support the second of these two alternative answers, and it was also a text which might seem to have been directly addressed to the Vicar of Peter.

The question presented itself in an urgent practical form to the would-be reformer Pope Gregory VI when he assumed the burden of the Papal office in A.D. 1045. In order to serve as the instrument of reform, the Holy See must be efficiently organized; to be organized, it must have money; and the necessary supplies of this material means to a spiritual end were not forthcoming; for, while the old Papal revenues from the Patrimonia Petri had disappeared with the Patrimonia themselves, the new revenues arising from the offerings of the pilgrims were being stolen from the very altar of Saint Peter's own church by the brigand-nobles of the Ducatus Romanus—the one place in Western Christendom where the Prince of the Apostles had no honour, just because it was the country which he had made his own. No one would dispute that this sacrilegious robbery was as wicked in itself as it was damaging to the interests of the Papacy and the Christian Republic; and there was no prospect of the criminals becoming amenable to spiritual appeals or spiritual censures. The physical force which they themselves were employing was the only human agency to which they would yield. Was it justifiable to meet force with force in this flagrant case? The question was answered when the gentle Giovanni Graziano ascended the Papal throne as Gregory VI and appointed Hildebrand to be his *capellanus;* for the guardianship of Saint Peter's altar, with the gifts that were heaped upon it, was the *capellanus's* principal duty, and Hildebrand promptly fulfilled it by raising an armed force and routing the brigands *manu militari* [with an armed force].

In taking this first momentous step in his career the Papal *capellanus* was making Muhammad's response to a challenge that had confronted the Arabian prophet in his native city of Mecca. Like Muhammad in Mecca in the seventh century of the Christian Era, Hildebrand in Rome in the eleventh century had to cope with the problem of performing a spiritual task in a political vacuum, and, in support of a solution in which he was unwittingly following an Islamic precedent, Hildebrand could have quoted Christian Scripture for his purpose. He could have quoted to the brigands "my house shall be called the house of prayer, but ye have made it a den of thieves," and quoted to the Pope "the zeal of thine house hath eaten me up." But which of the scenes in the mystery play was Hildebrand really acting? Was he playing the part of Jesus when he "made a scourge of small cords" and "went into the Temple of God and cast out all them that sold and bought in the Temple and overthréw the tables of the moneychangers"? Or was he doing in fact what Jesus had been falsely accused of doing when the Pharisees said "this fellow doth not cast out devils but by Beelzebub the prince of the devils"?

At the moment when Hildebrand took action the inward moral character of his act was difficult indeed to divine. At his last hour, forty years after, the answer to the riddle was already less obscure; for in A.D. 1085, when he was dying as a Pope in exile at Salerno, the more venerable city that was his see lay prostrate under the weight of an overwhelming calamity which her bishop's policy had brought upon her only the year before. In 1085 Rome had just been looted and burnt by the Normans—more ferocious brigands than any native Roman breed—whom the Pope had called in to assist him in a mili-

tary struggle which had gradually spread from the steps of Saint Peter's altar, where it had started forty years before, until it had engulfed the whole of Western Christendom. The climax of the physical conflict between Hildebrand and Henry IV gave a foretaste of the deadlier and more devastating struggle which was to be fought out *à outrance* between Innocent IV and Frederick II; and by the time when we come to the pontificate of Innocent IV our doubts will be at an end. Sinibaldo Fieschi bears witness against Ildebrando Aldobrandeschi that, in choosing the alternative of meeting force by force, Hildebrand was setting the Hildebrandine Church upon a course which was to end in the victory of his adversaries the World, the Flesh, and the Devil over the City of God which he was seeking to bring down to Earth. . . .

. . . between 1353 and 1367, when the republican movement in Rome had been discredited—after two centuries of licence—by the antics of Rienzi, and when civic liberties were on the wane all over Central and Northern Italy, a Spanish soldier, Cardinal Albornoz, made an effective conquest of the greater part of the Donation of Charlemagne on behalf of a Papal master who was then still hugging the golden chains of a humiliating "Babylonish Captivity;" and at the turn of the fourteenth and fifteenth centuries, at the height of the Great Schism, Albornoz's work was repeated and confirmed by Pope Boniface IX with one hand, while with the other hand he was contending with his rival Benedict of Avignon. In the course of the next hundred years these Italian possessions of the Papacy became securely welded together into one of the ten despotically governed principalities into which the sixty or seventy medieval city-states of Central and Northern Italy were consolidated during the transition from the Medieval to the Modern Age. In this one field the Papacy achieved, in its decline, a success which had never come its way in the period of its Hildebrandine greatness; and the achievement was not undone, or even interrupted, by a series of unprecedented disasters: the "Babylonish Captivity" of 1309–76, the Great Schism of 1378–1417, the Reformation, and the Sack of Rome in 1527. The reason was that the erection of the Papal principality was an almost automatic consequence of the establishment of a new international order—or anarchy—in the Western World; and in yielding to this new dispensation, which was an utter reversal of the Hildebrandine regime, the Papacy was simply allowing itself to drift on an irresistible tide which was not, this time, of the Papacy's own raising. The modern Papal State was one of the Machiavellian secular "successor-states" into which the Hildebrandine ecclesiastical commonwealth was partitioned; and it lasted as long as the rest of the territorial system of which it was part and parcel—maintaining itself on the Rhône till A.D. 1791 and on the Tiber till A.D. 1870.

The consciousness that it was now drifting with the tide, and that it had lost control over its own destinies, was no doubt the psychological cause of the conservatism to which the Papacy abandoned itself from the time when it received the shock of the Protestant Reformation until the time when it began to recover from the later shock which was administered to it by the Italian *Risorgimento*.[1] Realizing that it was now at the mercy of wind and wave, the Papacy came to see its safety in stagnation.

[1] *Risorgimento:* nineteenth-century war of national unification.—Ed.

When thou wast young, thou girdedst thyself and walkedst whither thou wouldest; but when thou shalt be old thou shalt stretch forth thy hands, and another shall gird thee and carry thee whither thou wouldest not.

For a person or institution that has come to this pass, any change is formidable, because it will not be a change that is voluntary, and may be a change for the worse. It was in this spirit that the Papacy set its face, not only against the hierarchical and theological innovations of the Protestant Reformation, which were deliberately antagonistic to the Hildebrandine order of society, but also against some of the new discoveries of modern Western Physical Science and new ideas of modern Western Social Philosophy.

We have now perhaps found some answer to the question how the Papacy came to suffer its extraordinary περιπέτεια; but in describing the process we have not explained the cause. We may be justified in our thesis that the downfall of the Papacy in every sphere can be traced back to its abandonment of the spiritual in favour of the material sword, and that this fatal change can be traced, in its turn, to Hildebrand's choice in the first act of his public life. Yet, even if it were demonstrable that Hildebrand's decision in A.D. 1045 to parry force with force was the ruin of the Hildebrandine enterprise as a matter of fact, this would not prove that what did happen was bound to happen *a priori*. The single example of the Hildebrandine tragedy, impressive though it may be, can prove no more, in itself, than the truism that the use of material means towards a spiritual end is always a dangerous game. To live dangerously, however, is the inevitable condition of being alive at all; and there is no decisive evidence for the operation of a moral Gresham's Law to make it certain that, whenever force is employed in a spiritual cause, this dangerous manoeuvre will always incur defeat. There may be cases in which the same manoeuvre can be resorted to with a chance of success, and some cases, perhaps, among these, in which no other line of action holds out any prospect of victory, so that there the choice will lie between risking defeat in a hazardous move and accepting defeat without a struggle. In fact, notwithstanding the experience of the Hildebrandine Church, this Riddle of the Sphinx remains inscrutable still. And in our own later generation, when we find ourselves confronted once more by Hildebrand's dilemma, with the advocates of an uncompromising pacifism arrayed *ancipiti Marte* [indecisively] against the advocates of enforcing peace, we cannot pronounce that Hildebrand's choice was intrinsically the wrong one simply because it resulted in a disaster in Hildebrand's case. It is therefore not enough to show how this disaster occurred; we have also to answer, if we can, the question why.

Why was it that the medieval Papacy became the slave of its own tools, and allowed itself to be betrayed, by its use of material means, into being diverted from the spiritual ends to which those means had been intended to minister? In the history of the Roman See, as in that of the Roman Republic, the explanation of an ultimate defeat is to be found (so it would seem) in the untoward effects of an initial victory. The dangerous game of fighting force with force had in these cases fatal results because, to begin with, it succeeded only too well. Intoxicated by the successes which their hazardous manoeuvre obtained for them in the earlier stages of their struggle with the Holy Roman Empire, Pope Gregory VII and his successors persisted in the use of force,

and carried it to extremes, until it defeated the users' purpose by becoming an end in itself. While Gregory VII fought the Empire with the object of removing an Imperial obstacle to a reform of the Church, Innocent IV fought the Empire two hundred years later with the object of breaking the Imperial Power. The downfall of the Hildebrandine Papacy was a supremely tragic performance of the drama of κόρος-ὕβρις-ἄτη.[2]

We can verify the working out of this *Leitmotiv* in two ways. We can discern it in a contrast between some earlier and some later scene in the play; and we can detect it by an analysis of the plot.

The first pair of outwardly similar but inwardly diverse scenes is one in which three rival claimants to the Papacy are summoned before the judgement-seat of a council of the Church under the presidency of a Holy Roman Emperor, with the result that two of them are declared illegitimate, the third is permitted to avoid deposition by abdicating, and the Holy See thus rendered vacant is filled in due course by the election of a new candidate. In A.D. 1046 it was Pope Gregory VI who was compelled by the Emperor Henry III to abdicate, at the Synod of Sutri, in order to make way for Suidger of Bamberg to ascend the Papal throne as Clement II; in A.D. 1415 it was Pope John XXIII who was compelled to abdicate by the Fathers of the Council of Constance, under the auspices of the Emperor Sigismund, in order that Oddone Colonna might become Pope Martin V. Externally the two scenes might seem almost indistinguishable, but there is a difference in ethos between the two pro-

---

[2] *Koros:* arrogance by virtue of success; *hybris:* loss of moral perspective through *koros; ate:* catastrophic and irresistible impulse, brought on by hybris, to attempt the impossible.—Ed.

tagonists which gives some measure of the moral disaster to which the Papacy had succumbed in the course of the four intervening centuries. Pope Gregory VI was an unworldly saint who had rendered himself technically guilty of the offence of Simony by purchasing the Papal office, with money legitimately acquired, in order to rescue it from the hands of his unworthy god-son, Pope Benedict IX. The offence had been so strictly formal, and the motive so plainly pure, that John Gratian's action had been acclaimed by Peter Damian as the salvation of the Church, while Hildebrand showed his opinion of it by taking service under his old schoolmaster as his *capellanus* and assuming this master's pontifical name when his own turn came, long afterwards, to ascend the Papal throne as Gregory VII. The condemnation of Gregory VI was a travesty of justice· which aroused indignation all over Western Christendom and inspired Hildebrand to devote his life to fighting for the liberation of the Church from an arbitrary "Caesaropapism." Yet the victim of this judicial act of injustice accepted and endorsed the sentence without a murmur. Not so the condottiere Baldassare Cossa, "the most profligate of Mankind," whom the Council of Constance had to deal with as Pope John XXIII. "He fled, and was brought back a prisoner; the most scandalous charges were suppressed; the Vicar of Christ was only accused of piracy, murder, rape, sodomy, and incest; and, after subscribing his own condemnation, he expiated in prison the imprudence of trusting his person to a free city beyond the Alps." The poison of worldliness had worked potently in the course of less than four hundred years to produce the contrast between this scene and that. . . .

. . . in playing their part as fifteenth-

century Italian despots, the Popes became steeped in that pride of life which was the dominant note of the medieval Italian culture in its fifteenth-century over-ripeness. In this generation and this mood a Rodrigo Borgia on the Papal throne out-heroded a Baldassare Cossa; and, once again, the fox was caught. Within less than a hundred years after the dissolution of the Council of Basel in 1449 the Papacy was in even worse case than it had been in when the Council of Constance had opened in 1414. The Pope had defeated the Conciliar Movement to his own undoing. "He made a pit and digged it, and is fallen into the ditch which he made."

After the turn of the fifteenth and sixteenth centuries the power which the Papacy had refused to share constitutionally with a parliament of the Christian Commonwealth was lawlessly snatched out of its hands by the parochial secular princes, who might have been kept within bounds by the oecumenical authority of a Pope in Council, but who now found an easy prey in a Pope who alienated and disillusioned the *Plebs Christiana* by recklessly setting his own will to power against the people's yearning for reform and relief. The Papacy had rebuffed the Conciliar Movement as Rehoboam once rebuffed the congregation of Israel, and the same consequences followed.

The king answered the people roughly, and . . . spake to them . . . saying: "My father made your yoke heavy, and I will add to your yoke; my father also chastised you with whips, but I will chastise you with scorpions." . . . So when all Israel saw that the king hearkened not unto them, the people answered the king saying: "What portion have we in David? Neither have we inheritance in the son of Jesse. To your tents, O Israel. Now see to thine own house, David." So Israel departed unto their tents—

and in every tent they found some Henry Tudor who was eagerly waiting for his opportunity to play Jeroboam's part. It was by licence of the disillusionment of a popular feeling which had tried and failed to rally round the Papacy in the Conciliar Movement that the parochial princes could venture with impunity, a century later, to rise up against the Papacy and despoil it.

The losses of power that were inflicted on the Papacy in the sixteenth century were staggering.

As an Italian territorial sovereign the Pope now saw himself dwarfed, as hopelessly as his peers the Grand Duke of Tuscany and the Signoria of Venice, by the rising Transalpine and Transmarine Powers. It was in vain that he had welded Tivoli and Viterbo onto Rome, and Umbria and the Marches onto the Agro Romano, and the Legations onto the Marches. A Papal principality which had extended itself from the Tyrrhene Sea to the Adriatic and from the Garigliano to the Po might be a Great Power in Italy, but it was a pygmy in a new world which contained the France of Louis XI and the England of Henry VII and the Spain of Ferdinand and Isabella. After attempting to strut in arms on this giant's stage, and exposing itself to such humiliating experiences as its war of A.D. 1556–7 with King Philip II of Spain, the Papacy learned the lesson which Athens learned in the Chremonidean War, and withdrew as far as possible from active participation in an international war-game which it had found too boisterous. But this tardy Papal recognition of the drawbacks of territorial sovereignty did not save Pope Innocent XI from being bullied by Louis XIV or Pope Pius VII from being dragged at the chariot-wheels of Napoleon.

While the Pope suffered this fate as an Italian secular prince, he suffered still more grievous misfortunes as the oecumenical sovereign of the Western Church. In this latter capacity he saw the whole of his power reft away from him in the states that turned Protestant, and four-fifths of it in those that professedly remained Catholic—for their Catholic Majesties were not less rapacious than their Protestant Majesties in robbing the Papacy of its powers for their own benefit; the only difference in their policy was that they left the Papacy in possession of that fraction of its powers which, in the countries that turned Protestant, was abandoned by the prince to his subjects as a prison-yard exercise-ground for the individual conscience.

These sixteenth-century blows were the nemesis of the Papacy's fifteenth-century relapse into ὕβρις; but they were also the stimulus of a sixteenth-century revival. In this extremity the Catholic Church was snatched from the jaws of destruction by the very present help of a band of saints who utterly eclipsed the respectable but prosaic fathers of Constance and Basel, and whose like had not been seen in Western Christendom since Saint Louis had died in 1270 on the last crusade and Saint Thomas in 1274 on his way to the Council of Lyon. Saint Ignatius Loyola (*vivebat* A.D. 1495–1556) captured the intellectual prowess of Italy, which had ministered to a Papal pride of life when a Giovanni de' Medici was reigning as Pope Leo X, and bent it to the service of reform by yoking it with a Janissarian discipline. Saint Teresa (*vivebat* A.D. 1515–82) and Saint John of the Cross (*vivebat* A.D. 1542–91) restored the lapsed austerities of the Carmelite Order and found their way through this door into a new world of mystical illumination. Saint Philip Neri (*vivebat* A.D. 1515–95) set a new standard of loving-kindness towards the poor and the sick, and a new standard of devotion for the ministry of secular priests. Saint Charles Borromeo (*vivebat* A.D. 1538–84) wholly succeeded, where Pope Innocent III had half failed, in performing the exacting task of an ecclesiastical administrator. Saint Francis de Sales (*vivebat* A.D. 1567–1622) was as intrepid a missionary of the Catholic Faith in the Protestant lion's den at Geneva as Saint Franics Xavier (*vivebat* 1506–52) was among the heathen in the Indies. These super-human men and women worked a work in our Western World which is still operative to-day and which has perhaps not yet begun to bear its richest fruits. In their own age, however (if it is not sheer nonsense for historians to pin down saints within temporal bounds) the dead weight of the Papal tradition brought the sixteenth-century saints' impetuous advance to a premature halt. They liberated the Papacy from the pride of life, but its lust for power proved too strong for them; and so the sixteenth-century rally failed, after all, to save the day. In the seventeenth century the Roman Church relapsed into a spiritual torpor which awoke into a counter-revolutionary activity—both political and intellectual—when it was stirred by the impact of an eighteenth-century Philosophy and a nineteenth-century Physical Science; and by the three hundredth anniversary of Saint Ignatius's death a Papacy which had once been the heart of the Western body social seemed to have become an atrophied member, in which the blood no longer coursed and the life no longer throbbed. The pontificate of Pius IX (*fungebatur* A.D. 1846–78), who saw the territorial sovereignty of the Papacy extinguished when the armed forces of the Kingdom of Italy entered Rome in 1870, marked as abysmal a fall in the fortunes of the Holy See as the pontificate of Clement VII (*fungebatur* A.D. 1523–34), who saw Rome sacked in 1527

by the Protestant mercenaries of the Emperor Charles V, or the pontificate of John XXIII (*fungebatur* A.D. 1410–15), who was brought to book at Constance.

As we read this tale of rout and rally and relapse which brought so great an institution so low in the course of some six hundred years, we shall be struck by a series of signal failures to learn from experience. Hildebrand himself, who had obtained his opportunity because the Emperor Henry III had overplayed a strong hand in 1046, made precisely Henry III's mistake when, thirty years later, he overplayed his own strong hand in dealing with Henry IV. Innocent III, as we have seen, was not deterred by the deplorable outcome of the Fourth Crusade from launching his crusade against the Albigenses with equally deplorable consequences; and the exposure of his credulity towards Otto Welf did not put him on his guard against Frederick II. Innocent IV did not perceive that the Holy See would be as much at the mercy of a King of Sicily who was brother to the King of France as it had been at the mercy of a King of Sicily who was himself the King of Germany—though the essential danger lay in being taken between two fires, without its making any substantial difference whether the Transalpine fire was German or French. Boniface VIII did not apprehend that if an insistence upon legal pretensions insufficiently supported by material power had been fatal to the Emperor Frederick I in his dealings with the Lombard communes, it would be equally fatal to Pope Boniface in dealing with the Kingdom of France. A Martin V and a Eugenius IV, when they set themselves to frustrate the Conciliar Movement, did not remind themselves that King Philip IV of France and King Edward III of England had deliberately fortified themselves with parliamentary support before their successful defiance of the Papacy in the fourteenth century, and therefore did not draw the statesman-like inference that an oecumenical parliament of the Western Ecclesiastical Commonwealth, so far from being a menace to the Pope's authority, was likely to be a tower of strength to him in a coming struggle with the parochial secular princes. A Julius II did not reflect that a pagan virtuosity in arts and arms, which had not saved from destruction the Papacy's arch-enemy Frederick II, was unlikely to bring salvation to the power by which Frederick had been conquered. And, in general, the experience of the Papacy in the fifteenth and sixteenth centuries in its encounters with the Renaissance and the Reformation did not make it any the more expert in dealing, in the eighteenth and nineteenth centuries, with the new forces of Democracy and Physical Science which had been generated by a fresh eruption of the Western social volcano.

As we contemplate this record of flood-lit truths unheeded and golden opportunities untaken, we cease to wonder at the unparalleled series of calamities by which the Hildebrandine Papacy has been afflicted in the long agony of its decline and fall: "the Babylonish Captivity," the Great Schism, the Protestant Reformation, the Italian *Risorgimento.* Are these the final fruits of the tree which Hildebrand planted? If so, the nemesis of creativity surpasses itself when it takes the form of the intoxication of victory.

The tragedy of the Hildebrandine Papacy is the tragedy of Periclean Athens. Athens became the oppressor of her sister city-states whom she had liberated from the oppression of the Achaemenidae; the Roman See became the oppressor of her sister churches whom she had lib-

erated from the oppression of the Secular Power in Western Christendom. In both tragedies the protagonist inverts his role; in both, the change is the outward visible sign of an inward spiritual debacle; and, in both, this mortal sin is visited with a condign punishment. In the Hellenic drama the devastation which the sin and the punishment deal does not stop short at the affliction of the victims and the abasement of the villain of the piece; it takes its course until it brings about the breakdown of the whole civilization in whose life the actors are playing their parts. In our Western drama, in which we ourselves are actors as well as spectators, are the sin and punishment of the Hildebrandine Papacy destined to bring the history of Western Christendom to the same tragic ending?

As we gaze round our spiritually devastated world in our generation, we can take the measure of the evil which has been brought upon us by the Hildebrandine failure now that its consequences have had nearly seven centuries to work themselves out since Innocent IV fought his Hannibalic War. And in the light of this latter-day knowledge we can see that the Hildebrandine Papacy's greatest crime against our Western Society has been, not its extermination of the Hohenstaufen or its assassination of the Conciliar Movement, but its felony against itself. In committing those crimes the Papacy did its best to commit suicide; and in dealing itself this prostrating blow it has left the house vacant for the entry of seven—and seventy times seven—other spirits who are all more wicked than the supplanted householder. In the four hundred years that have now been added to the tale of Western history since the outbreak of the Reformation the sins of Jeroboam have far surpassed the sins of the degenerate scion of David's house who gave the usurper his chance to seize nine-tenths of the Kingdom.

And Jeroboam said in his heart: "Now shall the kingdom return to the house of David. If this people go up to do sacrifice in the house of the Lord at Jerusalem, then shall the heart of this people turn again unto their lord, even unto Rehoboam King of Judah; and they shall kill me and go again to Rehoboam king of Judah." Whereupon the king took counsel and made two calves of gold, and said unto them: "It is too much for you to go up to Jerusalem; behold thy gods, O Israel, which brought thee up out of the Land of Egypt." And he set the one in Bethel, and the other put he in Dan. And this thing became a sin. . . .

The golden calves which our latter-day Jeroboams have set up in our Western World are called "totalitarian states"; and these are the gods which they invite— nay, command—us to worship in place of the God of Benedict and the God of Gregory and the God of Hildebrand and the God of Francis. To-day these false prophets of an odious idolatry sit in Hildebrand's seat. But their mandate is not inexhaustible, and, by the same token, our own doom is not sealed.

The cup of these usurpers' iniquities has run over in a generation which has seen the Papacy drink its own cup of humiliation to the dregs. On the 20th September, 1870, the wheel of Destiny completed its Great Year by coming round, full circle, to the pre-Hildebrandine situation of the 20th December, 1046. In the long flood of adversity the ὕβρις that was the Holy See's undoing has perhaps at last been washed away, and already history has begun to repeat itself. When the blow which was dealt to the Roman Church by a militant Italian nationalism in 1870 was immediately followed in a militantly nationalist Germany

by the launching of the *Kulturkampf*,[3] it almost seemed as though the last hour had struck for the Catholic Faith; yet that bloodless war of attrition on German soil ended in the first victory which the Church had gained for three hundred years—and this in a conflict with Bismarck, the most redoubtable Jeroboam of the age. Nor was the Catholic Church defeated in the struggle with state-worship in France which broke out in 1904. So far from that, it was becoming apparent in the fourth decade of the twentieth century that in France the future lay, not with the anti-religious ideas in the Ideology of 1789, but with the spiritual influence of the lives of a nineteenth-century band of saints whom the challenge of the French Revolution had called into action in France and Piedmont, as the sixteenth-century saints had been called into action in Spain and Italy and Savoy by the challenge of the Reformation. In Saint Jean-Baptiste Vianney, the curé d'Ars (*vivebat* A.D. 1786–1857), there was an epiphany of sainthood in the life of a parish priest; in Don Giovanni Bosco (*vivebat* A.D. 1815–88) there was an epiphany in the life of a "social worker"; in Saint Bernadette Soubirous of Lourdes (*vivebat* A.D. 1844–79) there was an epiphany in the life of a child of the Proletariat; in Saint Thérèse Martin, "the Little Flower" (*vivebat* A.D. (1873–97), there was an epiphany in the life of a child of the Bourgeoisie. This outburst of sainthood in the continental strongholds of a nineteenth-century secularism was the movement from the depths which was reflected on the surface of life in the successful resistance of the Church, as an institution, to

---

[3] *Kulturkampf*: nineteenth-century idea that there must be a struggle for the integrity of German national culture against international forces, especially the Papacy.—Ed.

the assaults of the German state *post* 1871 and of the French state *post* 1904. In the year 1938 it looked as though the victor in those preliminary skirmishes were now going into action in a pitched battle in which the whole strength of either side might be engaged; and in this conflict, if it was indeed at hand, the fate of Western Christendom would once more be in the balance.

At this hour of decision it is meet and right that all men and women in the Western World who "have been baptized into Christ" as "heirs according to the promise"—and, with us, all the Gentiles who have become "partakers of" the "promise" and "fellow heirs of the same body" through the adoption of our Western way of life—should call upon the Vicar of Christ to vindicate the tremendous title which Pope Innocent III has bequeathed to subsequent successors of Saint Peter. Did not Peter's Master say to Peter himself that "unto whomsoever much is given, of him shall be much required, and to whom men have committed much, of him they will ask the more"? To the Apostle at Rome our forefathers committed the destiny of Western Christendom, which was the whole of their treasure; and when "that servant, which knew his Lord's will", "prepared not himself, neither did according to his will," and was beaten, in just retribution, "with many stripes", those blows fell with equal weight upon the bodies of "the menservants and maidens" whose souls had been entrusted to the keeping of the *Servus Servorum Dei* [Servant of the Servants of God].

Quidquid delirant reges plectuntur Achivi.
Seditione, dolis, scelere atque libidine et ira
Iliacos intra muros peccatur et extra.[4]

The punishment for the ὕβρις of the servant who has said in his heart "My lord delayeth his coming" has been visited upon us; and it is for him who has brought us to this pass to deliver us from it, whosoever we may be: Catholics or Protestants; Christians or men of other faiths; believers or unbelievers; bond or free.

They were scattered because there is no shepherd, and they became meat to all the beasts of the field when they were scattered.

David has no defence against Eliab's taunt. Yet who but this very David, who has once deserted his flock, has the strength and hardihood to beard and smite and slay the lion and the bear and to deliver the lamb out of his mouth? Will our truant David once more take the field, to gather what Rehoboam has scattered and unite what Jeroboam has divided? And if, at a zero hour when all is sin and shame, a second Hildebrand does come to the fight and the rescue, will our deliverer this time be fore-armed, by the wisdom that is born of suffering, against that fatal intoxication of victory which has ruined the great work of Pope Gregory VII?

---

[4] [Whatever folly the kings commit, the Greeks suffer./ By sedition, plots, crime and lust and wrath,/ Wrong is done inside Ilium's walls and beyond them.—Ed.]